Jennifer,

Welcome to the Agency!

Here's to bringing
out the Celebrity
in you

CELEBRITY BRANDING YOU®

By JW Dicks, Esq., Nick Nanton, Esq., Lindsay Dicks and Greg Rollett

2nd Edition

Published by CelebrityPress®, Orlando, FL
A division of The Celebrity Branding Agency®

Celebrity Branding® is a registered trademark
Printed in the United States of America.

ISBN: 978-0-9886418-4-6
LCCN: 2013933740

This publication is designed to provide accurate and authoritative information with regard to the subject matter covered. It is sold with the understanding that the publisher is not engaged in rendering legal, accounting, or other professional advice. If legal advice or other expert assistance is required, the services of a competent professional should be sought. The opinions expressed by the authors in this book are not endorsed by CelebrityPress® and are the sole responsibility of the author rendering the opinion.

Most CelebrityPress® titles are available at special quantity discounts for bulk purchases for sales promotions, premiums, fundraising, and educational use. Special versions or book excerpts can also be created to fit specific needs.

For more information, please write:
CelebrityPress®
520 N. Orlando Ave, #2
Winter Park, FL 32789
or call 1.877.261.4930

Visit us online at: www.CelebrityPressPublishing.com

10 9 8 7 6 5 4 3 2 1

*To Linda, my wife, partner
and best friend for 40 years!*

*To Kristina, Brock, Bowen and Addison...
the real celebrities in my life.*

*To Eric, my husband, for your undying love
and unwavering support.*

*To my wife, Jennifer, and son, Colten,
the reasons I get up every day.*

Brian Tracy
Brian Tracy International, LLC (Solana Beach, CA)

"Not only is Nick a great guy; he's a great business partner as well. He's the top agent for celebrity speakers like myself. He helps us get better known so that we can charge more money and charge it more often.

Nick and the Dicks + Nanton Agency team also worked with great friends of mine like Dan Kennedy, Jeff Walker, Mari Smith and Ron LeGrand along with many, many more. What they do is help you to maximize your brand and your income by making people see you as special, different and more valuable than your competitors. They also help experts create a platform and elevate them to celebrity expert status in their fields.

Nick is the best in the world at what he does, and he's one of the most high-integrity guys myself and my team have ever worked with. If you're looking for an agent to maximize your celebrity status, your business and your income, Nick is your guy. Nick is our guy."

Sydney Barrows (New York, NY)

"I'm in awe of what an incredible job you and your team at the Dicks + Nanton Agency do in helping so many people realize their dream of having a best-selling book. It's a big deal to simply have a book published in the first place, but no other publisher I've ever worked with (and I've had four books published so far) has ever made it their business to actually get it on the best-seller list!

Your team is just wonderful; congratulations to you for having such a great group of talented and really-on-top-of-everything folks. They made it so easy! And somehow each one had the uncanny ability to make you feel like you were their only client and that nothing mattered more than getting your copy edited perfectly, your cover looking even better than you ever imagined it would, your e-book and a jpeg of the cover ready to be put up for sale on your website and in your hands right away, hardcopies of your books printed and shipped to you, and when the book hit No. 1, a certificate arrived ready to be framed, or even better, you can have one framed for you!

Each and every one of the Dicks + Nanton Agency team members was a pleasure to work with, and I'm just so thrilled to have had such a great experience and such a wonderful opportunity to get my message out there and in the hands of prospective clients in the form of the best authority-affirming method there is—a beautifully and professionally published book.

Jack Canfield (Santa Barbara, CA)
Best-Selling Author, Chicken Soup
for the Soul Series

"I love working with Nick and his team at the Dicks + Nanton Agency. They can absolutely help you get to the next level. Nick does everything he promises and then some!"

Daniel J. Liebrecht (Toledo, OH)

"Synergy. That's what you get with JW Dicks, Nick Nanton and the entire team at CelebrityPress®. And synergy is what you need if you want your book effectively <u>positioned, printed and promoted</u>. Because it's a lot more than printing.

We went from simply an idea to a clearly targeted finished product faster and with less hassle than we thought possible. From strategy and theme to design and editing, CelebrityPress® brought together all the right people.

The result was much more than simply a published book but rather having a properly targeted and promoted tool, along with *Best-Selling Author* status, to dramatically increase our credibility with our potential clients. And for a lot less than the cost of traditional advertising.

The final product, our book, printed and delivered on time and on target… blew us away! You'll like working with these guys, and better yet, you'll <u>love</u> the results!"

Kenny Chapman (Grand Junction, CO)

"Yesterday I had a consulting engagement with JW Dicks and Nick Nanton. It was the most unbelievable experience. Before my consulting session, I was a little apprehensive, as many of us are when we think about hiring coaches or consultants. I was wondering, 'What am I going to get? Am I going to get what I expect? Is it going to be worth my time and value?' Well I'm here to tell you that the answer to all of those questions is YES, and I got tons of value.

I can't even put into words what I walked out of that room with yesterday. I had an expectation. I had a goal of what I wanted to receive from that session. It was exponentially worth more than what I paid. Wherever you're at in your career, whatever you're thinking about working on, whether it's improving your celebrity status, or improving your business, these are the guys to work with. Don't worry about the cost, make the call, get booked, work with them today, and it will positively impact your business and your life more than you can possibly expect."

Ted Thomas (Merritt Island, FL)

"Nick, Jack and Lindsay, out of all the years I've been in business, I've NEVER seen ANYONE offer the media, marketing and PR triple threat that you guys do. You guys are MASTERS! Thanks for all you've done and continue you to do for me to help me build my business!"

Richard Seppala

"When I met Nick and Jack, my business was called Total Census Solutions, which was relevant to the niche I first started in (Senior Housing), but to the rest of the world it was confusing and very forgettable. Just by reviewing my bio, before we even had much time to speak, Nick and Jack shot back a bunch of ideas about how my business was really centered around getting people the maximum ROI in their advertising, and spun out The ROI Guy brand for me. In the past two years since they helped me reinvent my brand, my business has taken off! Now everywhere I go, people call me the ROI Guy, which is fun; however, the most important thing is they also know where to call when they need solutions for tracking their marketing campaigns and getting the greatest ROI! Oh yeah, and they also like to have a bit of fun too!"

Contents

YOUR CELEBRITY
BRANDING®
INTRODUCTION

YOUR CELEBRITY BRANDING®
INTRODUCTION

Rule #1: People Buy People

The central premise of this book and business philosophy is based on a proven fact:

"People Buy People"

Your prospect and your customer would rather make their buying decisions based on you as a person instead of dealing with a company that has no face or personality. This fact has been proved to us time and time again. With more than 50 collective years of running businesses and being entrepreneurs in the real world, we have spent millions of dollars of our own money to develop and prove this fact. We have built, joint-ventured, coached and consulted with other businesses that are spending hundreds of millions of dollars because they know the powerful business truth that a person or personality attached to your business will make it grow faster and create more money for you.

Many of you, based on your own experiences in the marketplace, immediately understand the importance of the business principle behind the personality-driven business. Some of you will find this statement to be a surprise at first. Then, once you consider what it means as a potential opportunity for you, your eyes will be opened to a completely new way of marketing and operating your business.

A few of you, many of whom work for "big businesses" that run multimillion-dollar ads in slick magazines, won't have any idea of we're talking about and may even get a little indignant and want to argue the point. You believe in the big, corporate brand and institutional advertising. If this is you, then respectfully, let us suggest that you close the book and take it back to the bookstore. Since you have not read the book, exchange it for one on the *New York Times* bestseller fiction list and at least enjoy a great read—harsh but practical.

For the rest of you, including the non-believers, who are at least willing to keep an open mind, we welcome you. You are our people, and we welcome you to a fun way of building your business that will be both rewarding and profitable. Once you "get it," you will experience one of the true unfair advantages left in business today—a cost-effective way to eliminate your competition, or at least make them irrelevant. Why? Because the one thing you have going for you that no one can duplicate is YOU. This is important for businesses of all sizes. You can be successful without a "personality," but it's easier to capture market share if you have one, even if it's an invented one like Mickey Mouse or Harry Potter.

What we are going to do in this book is teach you about the importance of positioning yourself not just as a personality but a Celebrity Brand by becoming the "Celebrity Expert®" in your area of expertise and in the market you compete in, be it local or national. The Celebrity Expert® elevates your status one more level because we all love our personalities, and at this point, let me just ask you not to fight It. Being a Celebrity in your niche is less work and hassle than being a movie star, and it is still a lot of fun.

There are four stages of the Celebrity Branding® process, and each stage has its own benefits:

> Stage 1: Finding Your Niche
> Stage 2: Creating Your Brand
> Stage 3: Developing Your
> Celebrity Expert® Status
> Stage 4: Rollout–Expanding Your
> Celebrity Brand Business
> Stage 5: Develop an Exit Plan

Each of the five stages of our celebrity-branding process is a distinct and rewarding accomplishment in and of itself. Some of you will not yet have started your first level, and you will require a more compelling story and proof of concept before you begin the process. Some of you have already developed your expert status and are now ready to move on to Stage 4 and expand your brand nationally, gaining the enormous profit potential that a national rollout holds. All of you, regardless of your current level, will make more money from your business and be in a personal position to do more good for others if you embrace the strategies we show you.

A Celebrity Expert®, unlike an unknown expert, has a unique following of fans (enthusiastic customers, clients and prospects). This fan following also allows you, as the Celebrity Expert®, to focus that group's attention on positive causes and charities that you can help to be more successful in addition to your own business. That is a very big benefit of becoming a Celebrity Expert®.

If we've grabbed your attention in these first few paragraphs, please open your mind and get ready to experience one breakthrough after another as you embark on the journey we like to call "Celebrity Branding You®."

STAGE 1
Finding Your Niche

1

The Truth About Celebrity Branding®

●

The Truth About Celebrity Branding®

Andy Warhol, the successful American painter, said, "In the future, everyone will get their 15 minutes of fame." In truth, we Americans love our celebrities, and we are always creating new ones. This is becoming even more prevalent in our rapidly increasing "reality" culture of blockbuster television shows like "American Idol," "X-Factor," and "Dancing With the Stars." If you can become a celebrity, the world is yours, albeit hopefully for more than 15 minutes. American Idol has promoted its celebrity judges to cult status and incredible incomes.

According to *Forbes* magazine, Simon Cowell earns a reported annual salary of more than $36 million just for the American Idol TV show. That excludes everything he earns on the ownership of the show; the British version, "America's Got Talent;" and the "X Factor."

In our media, marketing, and PR agency, Celebrity Branding Agency® LLC, we have consistently seen the power of celebrity attachment to a product or service, and how it produces an increase in the acceptance and sale of the product or service a company is offering. Over the years, we have come to realize that the simple reason for this is that "people buy people." The buyer wants to connect with a person that they know, like and trust. By using a celebrity personality in the form of an expert, it enhances the acceptance and increases the value of the product or service to the buyer. Buyers become more involved with the whole process as they begin to identify with the Celebrity Expert®. This is true for every industry: doctors, dentists, attorney, chiropractor, entrepreneurs, coaches, life planners, fitness coaches, speakers, authors, teachers and many others, all of whom we represent.

Take a moment to think about some of your favorite products that are endorsed by celebrities. You have a positive impression of the product and the celebrity, don't you? The positive impression and loyal feeling is a part of the magic of attaching a celebrity to a product.

Now, shift your vision so you can see YOURSELF as the Celebrity Expert®, endorsing your own product or service. This is where the real breakthroughs of taking a proven idea and applying it to your own business to increase its revenue occur. By the way, while we would prefer you to be the Celebrity Expert® for your own business, you don't have to be. Many businesses have promoted a family member or loyal employee to this celebrity status for the business. So, if for some reason you don't desire to be the "front person," don't miss out on the power that personality can bring your business—and the attention your growing reputation can bring to the causes you like or want to support. Just look at what Jared did to bring attention to already successful Subway franchise.

How Can You Use This Knowledge to Help Your Product or Service Be More Successful?

Celebrity Branding® is not about becoming a "fake" celebrity. Celebrity Branding® is about discovering who you are and your specific expertise or position in your industry. You then build on that expertise by getting media and PR credibility as an expert in your field. Celebrity Branding® then allows you to market yourself to your target market in an exciting way that produces a response that your prospect notices and reacts to in the form of buying your product or service because you are the recognized expert. The buyer believes in you and values your reputation. The more you can personally connect, the more value you create with your buying group.

This connection has become more important with the power of social media because friends look to friends as their trusted source for recommendations. You want to take on that role with your growing fan base and become the one people think of to recommend, and you want to recommend others as well.

You can increase your status from "expert," because you are good at what you do, to "Celebrity Expert®" when the world learns about you. We accelerate that process for our clients by getting the word out faster. We also help our clients structure their product or service in a way that is welcomed in the marketplace and generates the highest-perceived value.

Who Are You?

To become a celebrity brand, you must discover and present yourself in a unique and compelling way. You must understand who your client or customer really is and what they need from you. Without understanding this basic core of building your brand, the business structure you build will be hollow and unsustainable. Even after you are successful at building your celebrity brand, you must be flexible to change and adapt to your market. Some of the most successful celebrities of all time, like Cher and Madonna, have been the best at adapting and changing with the times by reinventing themselves while constantly delivering what their target audience wanted. They are successful to a great degree because they never lost focus on their market and always fulfilled the needs and desires of their customers.

While we can't answer the "Who are you?" question for you, we often help our clients find the answer by looking at the things that we all seem to gloss over when we attempt to look at ourselves objectively. Here are a few questions that will help you figure this out:

- What skills do you have that people find interesting and ask you about?

- What led you to your current job status? Personal status? Financial status?

- When people refer business to you, what do they tell others about you? (If you don't know the answer to this question, ask!)

- Why do your clients continually return to you and your products or services?

- What do you do when providing your product or service that is different than "what everyone else does?"

There are many more questions like this, but you get the idea. We concentrate on the things that most people gloss over and say, "That's no big deal." In fact, we are here to tell you that it is a big deal. You got to this point in your life based on a series of events, some memorable, some forgettable, some great and some not so great, but all those events brought you to this moment in time and have had a lasting effect. No other individual in the world has the exact same story as you, so don't hide who you are and where you come from. That's what makes you unique! The key factor you need to pay attention to when "finding" your story is to allow an objective third party help you weed through the story, pull out the "fluff," and keep the "meat."

We know firsthand how hard it is to be objective about your own work, so every time we write something, we always turn it over to a team of trusted colleagues, family and friends for their opinion. That is also what we are able to do for our clients—help them be objective.

What Is Your Mission?

Once people know who you are, the next question the world wants answered is: "What is your mission?" In other words, "How can you help me?" That's really what it all boils down to. What is it that you do that makes life easier, better, more fun or profitable for your customers?

The easiest way to answer this question is by looking at an old marketing phrase: "Tell your prospects about benefits, not features." To understand this concept, let's look at a few examples:

Feature:	Benefit:
- Open 24 hours	- Come in when it's convenient for you!
- We offer many loan programs	- We can help you find a loan with the right payment options for you!
- We handle corporate law	- Let us handle your corporate paperwork so you can do what you do best: run your business and make more money.

You can see how telling someone about benefits can help them quickly identify "What's in it for me?" This breakthrough is necessary for a person to give you the opportunity to earn their business. By telling potential clients about benefits instead of features, you take the guess work out of trying to figure out how your product or service will benefit them; you simply tell them up front!

Who Is Your Target Market?

After you learn who you are and your mission, you must discover your target market. If you do not understand who your market is, then you will likely go broke trying to reach them. This is a very important point that many people don't understand.

The reason you'll go broke if you don't understand your target market is that in today's business world, marketing is one of the greatest expenses of any business. To keep this cost down, and more money in your pocket, you must be able to target your market as narrowly as possible so the dollars you allocate to marketing yield the greatest return on investment (ROI).

When selecting your target market, pick a market you feel passionate about. If you feel passionate about your business, it will be evident to your customer, and they will feel it, too. This feeling will, in turn, breed confidence in you and your product or service. Tony Robbins, the great motivational speaker, said, "Live your life with passion." Most people simply don't do this. Too often, businesspeople get in a rut and feel trapped in their business. This feeling drains you in many ways and always leads to frustration and unhappiness because you are no longer living with passion.

You are not alone if you have this feeling of being in a rut. We have experienced it too at different times in our careers. We have also known doctors who are tired of working with sick patients, and lawyers who cannot stand the thought of practicing law anymore. Often, this is a natural progression of life, but frequently it happens because people choose their area of specialty for the wrong reasons. Maybe it was for money. Maybe it was for a family member who always wanted a doctor in the family. Whatever the reason, time catches up with them. If that's you, then commit yourself to using this time to reinvent yourself, enjoy what you do, and re-energize yourself to live with passion and serve a target market that makes you feel alive.

Ask yourself these questions:

- What groups of people use your product or service now? Considerations include age group, financial status, goals and objectives.

- Which of these groups do you most enjoy working with? Relating to your group will make connecting with them personally easier. For example, financial planners often want the older and wealthier client, but is that the best place to build the strong connection, or is it with your age group that is moving quickly toward success but not quite there yet. Whichever group you chose is fine, but you would use a different style and marketing strategy to connect with the different target groups.

- Do you feel motivated and energized when you think of providing your product or service to this group of people? If you do, great. If you don't, it will be recognized and the connection will be very difficult to make. You just can't "fake it to make it"—and there's no reason to. Find the fit now.

Once you answer these questions, you may well have found your target market. If you haven't found the answer, then discuss it with a close friend who knows you best. Sometimes we all have trouble "seeing the forest for the trees," especially when the answer is right under our nose. In this case, there's nothing better than a loyal, objective observer.

What Does Your Market Want or Need?

People react to buying messages for one of two reasons— to get pleasure or to avoid pain. Think about it. Pretty simple really, these are the two predominant forces in how we react to products or services. We want to buy a car because it gives us pleasure. We go to a doctor to get well and ease pain.

If your product or service can do both, you are fortunate. A health club, for example, might help you feel better and avoid pain. It can also help you look better and give you pleasure. In the marketing they use, the health club would want to point out all of their benefits and how they are accomplished.

To be the most successful in your field, you need to help your clients understand what benefits they're getting from you. And as they're reaping the benefits, you should reinforce the benefits and the client's success. Rarely do business owners do this, but they should. If your clients aren't being reinforced in a positive manner, they lose the passion in whatever it is you're providing them. Have you heard the question, "What have you done for me lately?" Enough said.

Do you reinforce the benefits you offer throughout all your client communications? In later chapters, we will go into the various ways we suggest you stay in touch with your clients and prospects so you're always present in their lives.

We believe in using all of the many forms of communication available today, both online and in person. Personal contact doesn't necessarily mean "face-to-face," although that's often best. Today, more than ever, there are many options that are very close to the feel of personal communication but have a broader reach, such as seminars, teleseminars, webinars and special events. The more communication methods you use, the stronger the likelihood of connecting with the one your clients learn best from.

How Does Your Product or Service Fulfill Your Market's Needs?

The next step in your client development process is to analyze how your service fills the needs of your market. What will it do for them? This answer needs to be conveyed in the form of the specific benefits they will receive.

If your market wants to look younger, then the benefit you must demonstrate is that your product can do just that—make them look younger. Interestingly, the benefit must outweigh the cost (cost is a pain people want to avoid). So if your product makes them look younger but costs more than they feel they can afford in terms of time, money or some other tangible benefit, your sales won't be what you desire. The results (benefits) have to be worth the investment. The reason being, even if you have the most compelling marketing in the world, your customers will not return to do business with you because they won't feel you understand them if you don't show them they are getting real value for the price.

All of you sell a service that helps people make or save money. Our own book "Celebrity Branding You®" is an example of that type of product. If we ask people to buy a book for $25, and they make $25 using what they learn, will they be happy? Probably not, because the reader has also invested their time in reading the book. What if the information helps the reader to make 10 times the amount invested? Will that increase the satisfaction of their investment? Of course it would, and that is the balance point you have to find. Is the magic number five times invested capital? Ten times? Twenty times? There is no concrete answer, but whatever the number is that tips the scale for your market, once you find it, you will have a group of very happy clients beating a path to your door.

Remember, it does not have to be solely a monetary return; it can easily be a "quality of life" return. Often a person follows a favorite author from book to book. They buy not only because of the dollar-investment return but the quality of life enjoyment they get while reading the book. A key role in your job of developing your successful product or service is to find the "tipping point" on the balance beam your client walks on to begin to feel the value they receive is worth more than the cost. Then you must continue to put pressure on the value side of the bar.

STAGE 2
Creating Your Brand

2

What Is Your Brand?

2

What Is Your Brand?

Your brand is what makes you uniquely different from everyone else in your target market. When put into words, this is often referred to in marketing as your unique selling proposition (USP). Your brand should be readily identifiable so people can quickly say, "That is what I need, and that is the person I want to solve my need!"

5WH

Journalists are taught that the secret formula for writing a compelling article is to answer 5WH—who, what, when, where, why and how. This is the same with a brand. To have a good brand, you must answer the following questions to convey what you do for your target market:

- Who are you?
- What do you do, and what are the expected results?
- When can you do it, and how long will it take?
- Where do you perform your service?
- Why do you do it?
- How do you accomplish it?

Let us give you an example using our own business:

- **Who:** We are Dicks+Nanton Celebrity Branding Agency®. We use our names in the company name so clients immediately begin to identify with us as people, not just a company. We use our pictures extensively on our website and on the cover of this book because we, as people, are identifiers of the brand. In the case of this company, we added the word "Agency" because people associate agents with celebrities, and we represent our clients in this fashion. Note that the name we chose for the business is clear. The name isn't fancy, but you quickly know who we are and what we do. For the Dicks+Nanton Celebrity Branding Agency® LLC, we selected words that involve what we uniquely do: celebrity branding. The brand is unique and has a strong appeal.

- **What do we do, and what are the expected results:** We answer this in our slogan, "Celebrity Branding You®." Also, we use testimonials on our websites and in our marketing materials to reinforce what we do. Third-party testimonials are one of the most powerful tools you can use for demonstration purposes because interested readers will be more compelled to act based on what someone else says about you than what you say about yourself. Whenever you get the opportunity, let your clients talk about the results you produce.

- **When can you do it, and how long will it take:** Naturally, we aren't always available to immediately start working with a new client. That's one of the reasons we wrote this book. By reading and understanding our philosophy and process, many of you can do it on your own or perhaps just use us to help with a particular stage or process. This reduces the time to get results. If you are a client who is starting from scratch, the process of building your brand will take longer, but the results are worth the time. The time it takes to reach success is never quick enough, but the one thing we know is that the sooner you begin, the sooner you will achieve your goals.

• **Where do we perform our service:** While our services are available internationally we have a practical limitation on the number of clients we can personally handle at one time. However, thanks to technology, we can serve our clients anywhere. If you chose to be limited in your geography you should work that to your advantage by promoting it.

• **Why we do it:** This is the telling and sharing part of your story. In our case, we all live and breathe growing businesses of all types through personality-driven branding, and using media, marketing and PR to convey the brand to prospects. It's a formula few understand, but once they do, it totally changes their business. Having a message so strong and powerful gives us a mission that can help so many people.

• **How do we do what we do:** Many years ago we discovered that business is formulaic. If you learn the formula for a successful business, your business will grow. Please note that we did not say there will not be problems in your business, because there will be. All businesses face problems, and sometimes they cannot be resolved fast enough. We have experienced this personally and have seen some of our clients go through it. What we have learned from experience is that you must adapt to problems by finding creative solutions, and then return to the formula you were following. When you are in the eye of the hurricane, this is not easy to see. Clarity of vision is often a valuable service we give our clients—a view from the outside. Experience is a great teacher, but learning from someone who has been there and can keep you out of harm's way is a better and less painful plan.

"Celebrity Branding You®" is also formulaic. We have created a process that if followed will return the desired results. There are variations and nuances, but the basic formula is the same, and it works each time we follow it and in all different types of businesses and professions. It will work for you, too.

These are the answers to our own brand questions. We use the answers in all of our communications with clients and prospects. The more you share with people about yourself and your story, the faster they can make a personal decision about you and whether you will work well together. The ones who like our answers and business philosophy stay with us, and the ones who do not fire themselves before we get the chance. And yes, before you ask, we do fire clients. It is a MUST because quality of work is extremely important. Working with who you want and the people you can provide the greatest help to because of their openness to your ideas and strategies is what brings excitement and passion to your work. It also frees you to do what you do best. By concentrating on the connected client, you will perform better and the client will be happy because the results are better. This is a business truth that is difficult to see when you're getting started and want to put more food on the table. But the sooner you're able to structure your work around this business philosophy, the more you will be successful, both internally and externally.

3

Putting Your Story Behind Your Brand

Putting Your Story Behind Your Brand

Perhaps the single most important element to learn when creating a celebrity brand is to turn your inner personality outward to the public. You must learn to open up and let your market see who you are, warts and all. The more open and transparent you are about yourself, the stronger your brand becomes. Naturally, as you expose yourself, you will lose some people who decide you are not the person they want to work with because of their own reasons. This is hard to accept in the beginning because of the feelings we all have toward personal rejection. You have to overcome this feeling and accept the inevitable truth—you cannot please everyone, and you will be able to help more people in the long run that actually connect to you if you focus on the ones who accept you as you are. The more open you are with these people about who you are, the more accepting they will be to your proposition and the stronger your relationship will become. The Celebrity Experts® we know who are the best at this have created a network of raving fans who help each other accomplish a great deal more than anyone could do on their own. This is what we want for you.

Why Do You Do What You Do?

Have you ever asked yourself why? If you haven't, now is a good time to explore that question. If the answer is, "Because this is what I have always done," then it's likely that what you're doing may not make you happy. If you ask yourself the question, and you did not like the answer, then you are not satisfied either.

You don't have to be overjoyed with what you do, nor do you have to be happy all the time about what you do. In fact, everyone is unhappy from time to time because the circumstances make the moment unpleasant. This is different from being happy with what you are doing, and it is likely no one ever told you there was a difference.

Being happy with what you are doing means that your work has meaning for you. Because we spend so much time at it, having meaningful work is important. If you don't enjoy your work, you need to consider why and make the changes necessary to correct it. The more meaningful your work, the more you can use it to help others beyond yourself. In turn, you will find that the results make your work even more meaningful.

What Do People Talk to You About or Compliment You On?

The answer to this question generally leads to the answer about what you do best for others. When people come up to you and seek your advice, it shows that they have thought about you and decided you are the person who has the answer they need. They may be right or wrong, but if a pattern develops, then you know-how the world views what you do, and maybe who you are. They have put you into a category, and hopefully, that is where you want to be. If not, then you must discover why people perceive you in that particular light and find out how to alter that perception to be more in line with your beliefs.

This is a powerful message for you. Often, we fight what we are really good at because we don't think that's what we, want to do. However, it is frequently what we should be doing and are supposed to do as our place in this world. This is a conflicting and complicated issue well beyond this book, if only because it takes so much study to find the answers. However, it's something you should strongly pay attention to as life leads you—you just have to listen.

How Do You Communicate With Others?

This question isn't intended to address types of communication but the manner in which your communication is received by others. Have you ever received an email and thought the sender must be really mad, only to find out that wasn't true at all? We all have, and that's the real problem with the email society we live and work in today. We fire off emails without any thought as to how a person may perceive what we are saying. This is why it's important in emails, and other forms of communication, that we're careful about what we're conveying to the recipient. Great harm can be inflicted on a relationship simply because the other person reads "tone" in your email or your voice that wasn't intended.

Remember, in business, you are always on stage. Your customers, clients and prospects are always watching and processing, both consciously and unconsciously, what you say and do, even in your expressions and body language.

While this is not a course in salesmanship or the use of body language, we are talking about branding. What you say and what you do is part of that process, and if you aren't conveying what and how you want to be branded, people will brand you themselves. Once they brand you, it's very difficult to get them to change their perception, so analyze your movements and actions carefully.

What's Your Elevator Pitch?

Your *elevator pitch* is the essence of what you would tell someone about what you do if you stepped into an elevator and they asked. We all have an answer; the issue is whether what we say conveys the right information. Does your answer give the individual a potential benefit to them? If not, they may get out of the elevator without another thought about you as long as they live.

Let's say you were to get into an elevator with us and ask the question, "What do you do?" and we were to say, "we're attorneys" (which Nick and JW are). Good answer from a speed standpoint but not so good from a business standpoint. The reason is because the individual across from you is mentally going through the process of pigeonholing you into one of his brain's filing cabinets. The word "attorney" is easy to process, and we would be sent to your filing cabinet to decipher this word. Unfortunately, what we don't know is how the word attorney is perceived by this person. If they just got through a messy divorce, the title "attorney" may be well subtitled "jerk," and the relationship we had a chance of starting is ended rather abruptly.

In our case, such a response would be way off-base for our Celebrity Branding Agency®, and we might not ever connect with the client who might really need our help with branding, media, marketing and PR. What if instead of attorney we responded, "We help entrepreneurs and professionals become the recognized Celebrity Experts® in their field in order to grow their businesses faster.

Can you imagine the brain working fast to try and find a filing cabinet that holds corresponding information for that category? In most cases, they would not have a file, or the file for "Celebrity Expert®" would pop open and the individual would follow up with a question because it needs more input. The follow-up would be our invitation to provide more information that will interest this person and entice them to see how we can benefit them.

The elevator pitch is hopefully not the end of the conversation but only the beginning of a dialogue. If the conversation continues, then you have the opportunity to explain the benefits of what you have to offer. For example, if we know the person was in the financial services field, we would have said we help financial planners instead of helping entrepreneurs and professionals. Doing so would have made a faster connection with the other person.

If the prospect says something like, "Oh, how do you do that," then you've been given permission to provide more feedback, and you should be ready to continue by explaining further so their brain begins to fill the file cabinet associated with you.

In our case we might say, "We help our clients get recognized as the expert in their field by getting them on TV shows on ABC, NBC, CBS, and Fox affiliates around the country, and frequently get a book publishing deal so they can become a best-selling author in their field.

Usually, the response after this is something like, "Wow!"

because most people have no idea how to do this or even where to begin, so the dialog is usually sustained much longer than if we had just said we were an attorney, I can assure you.

The process of pigeonholing people goes on all day with people we meet in elevators and even more often at networking and social events. When it happens, you know the importance of being prepared. Having a statement to tell them what you do will either arouse more interest or convey a strong benefit to the other party, and will make them want to know you more. Having a strategy to begin an open dialogue by provoking the other person to actually think about what you do and the benefits you offer is the first step in getting them to think about how you can help them or someone they know.

It is also important that you decide where you want to be pigeonholed. We have all been taught at one point or another not to pigeonhole ourselves. This was bad advice at best. If a potential client doesn't know where to "file you away," then chances are you will be forgotten, and that client will never seek you out to do business with you. The prospect must put you in one of their "filing cabinets" or create one for you in order to be able to retrieve the information when they need to. In order for the prospect to find a use for your services, you must give them specific ideas about how they can benefit from doing business with you.

In order for people to find a use for your services, you must give them specific benefits and ideas about how they can benefit from doing business with you. Let's look at an example in the medical industry. How many brain surgeons do you know who are struggling to pay their rent? We doubt many are. But when someone asks them what they do, they may say, "I am a doctor" or "I am a brain surgeon." By choosing to be pigeon-holed in a narrower classification, they're able to be more readily identified by the person they just met. They also narrow their classification in that individual's mind—making them easier to recall if they ever need a brain surgeon.

STAGE 3

Developing Your
Celebrity Expert® Status

4

Building Your
Celebrity Expert® Image

4

Building Your Celebrity Expert® Image

Let's face it, we are all judged by the first impression we give to others. It would be nice if it weren't so, but that would be unrealistic. So let's just work within the parameters we know to be true.

Since people are going to make a judgment about you when they first meet you, then you must make that impression consistent with your brand. If your brand is formal, then you can't look too casual or people will have an initial impression of incongruence, which leads to disbelief. While you can overcome that first impression, why make it so hard on yourself?

One of our clients likes to be known as "The Blue-Jeans Broker." The reason is because she is in real estate and finds that she spends lots of time touring properties. She also is just a more casual and relaxed person. Consequently, she wears…blue jeans. Sometimes she dresses things up a notch by wearing a jacket, and she is always neat about her entire appearance. But when you see her, you know who she is and can instantly relate to her and her approach. Her look is congruent.

What Other Ways Can You Reinforce Your Message?

Building your brand image also extends to other ways people see or hear you. One of the first things we recommend to clients is to have a professional photographer take their photo. Don't just go down to the little camera booth at the fair and have some snapshots taken (unless that look and feel is congruent with your brand).

Also, don't just go for the "glamour" shots that are heavily promoted from time to time. "Glamour" shots are often so posed that they make you appear unapproachable or like someone who may be trying too hard. Just be who you are, and be warm and inviting as though you are talking to your best friend who you just reconnected with after 20 years. Do that, and your pictures will come across well.

While a big smile in your photograph makes sense, you won't believe how hard we have to fight our clients when they go through one of our Celebrity Branding® Experiences and get their photos taken at a professional photo shoot we put on. We recommend that you smile big, because in most cases, what is big to you, is softened by the camera, and once again, you miss an opportunity to connect with people who see your photo. It's said that the eyes are the window to the soul, and learning to use a big smile that uses your expressive eyes is the way to make the connection you want.

Your image also extends to your business cards, website, and other collateral material. We try and present our clients to their potential client base in as many different media as possible. The reason is because we all have different ways of connecting with people. For instance, think about how you like to learn new information. Is it by listening? Others prefer to read a book because they like to see words and, in some cases, feel the pages. For other people, both receptors, visual and auditory, are important. Still others like to just "see" the message. To best reach the largest number of people, you want your message presented in all different categories. For example, don't just hand out a business card; consider passing out a CD or DVD as well. If you write a book on your expertise, we would want to make sure your picture is on the cover of the book. When we publish our clients' books, we make sure that the image on the cover is consistent with their brand. Additionally, we recommend hard-cover books and even give a specially coated soft and elegant feel to the cover. Again, we do this because people take in information differently. To those who are visual, we want them to see you in a certain way. To others who are tactical in the way they receive information, we want them to feel the authority that a hard-cover book conveys and the soft, velvety fee of the specialized cover.

Now that you know that people are processing information about you differently, you'll see why it's important to have different processes for bringing people to you and ways to show them what you have to offer Publishing a book helps you reach certain groups of people. Putting on a seminar conveys your brand to an entirely different set of people who receive your information differently. *Using all forms of media and marketing channels opens the different doors to the many ways people can meet you and become involved with your services.*

You should also begin to see that growing a business means using many different marketing channels. Today, many new businesses try to use just email because it is free. While free can be good, it can also be expensive if your business fails because you don't reach your target audience. Some people won't even buy from email. The more marketing channels you use, the larger your prospect funnel will be. Casting a wider but targeted net helps you reach more of the very people who have a need for your service.

5

Building Your Credibility As A Celebrity Expert®

5

Building Your Credibility As A Celebrity Expert®

When we first talk to clients, some are reluctant to feature themselves as their brand because of internal credibility issues they perceive as a problem. In some cases, it has to do with a lack of a formal education. If this is a concern, you can eliminate it right now because the good news is that very few people care anymore.

At one time a formal education may have been important. Now, it isn't, and many a billionaire has dropped out to make his or her fortune, with Bill Gates, the richest man in the world, leading the list. Please don't use this as an excuse to drop out of school, but don't use it as a crutch either!

If you don't have a formal education, and you feel the need to have some educational credentials, then get certified in your specialty. While you can buy degrees from degree mills that sell them on the internet, this isn't what we recommend.

Write a Book

One of the best ways to gain credibility in your field is to write a book related to your expertise. At first, thinking about writing a book is a daunting task. A great way to start is by writing a series of articles on your chosen topic that will later form the chapters for your book. As you write each article or chapter, you can use it as a "special report" that can be used as a gift or handout to prospects.

When we wrote this book, we published many of the chapters as special reports before we completed the entire book. Each chapter was sent to our clients and prospects as we wrote them. Next, we used pieces of the chapters in our blogs and e-zines that we send to our clients. Since these are great ways to get instant information to clients and stay in touch with them, writing the chapters gave us good reasons to do so.

In addition to using the book chapters you write to stay in touch with your own circle of influence, you can also send out the chapters in the form of articles to article marketers on the internet. They promote them to other e-zine publishers looking for good material for their clients. More on this later, but for now you should understand that this is an amazing way to get your material out to the public. You also get a free byline and link to your website. This "free advertising" invites people to contact you for more information and check out your services. It's a great symbiotic relationship that everyone profits from. The e-zine or newsletter that you allow to publish your article gets good material, its readers benefit, and you get free promotion for your work. Better still, since your article is appearing in someone else's published work, it's essentially a testimonial, and that's one of the best forms of advertising. The publisher is telling their readers that they have given your work their "blessing," which is a very high form of endorsement you can't buy.

Testimonials

Testimonials are one of the best ways to build brand credibility. When you say you're great, it's perceived in a certain way—and not always positive. But when others tout you as an expert, it's different. Testimonials are perceived as the highest form of praise and endorsement.

Start building a testimonial file for yourself about you and your services as soon as possible. It's really not as hard as it seems, because in most cases, all you need to do is ask. Sometimes people do not give testimonials simply because they don't know what to say. This is easily resolved by giving them a quote about you and asking them if it is OK to use. You can also ask them a series of questions; the answers they give are testimonials.

Don't forget to also ask permission to use the testimonials people give you in your materials. Most people have no problem with this and are happy to help, but since some people don't like being exposed to the general public for whatever reason, it's always better to get approval in writing. You do not want to hear from your endorsers later in a lawsuit. Better to be safe than sorry, as they say!

Using audio and video testimonials can be even stronger than print, particularly on your website. Technology is making these audio or video testimonials easier to capture and post on your site. People like to see the people who are recommending you because it helps them make a personal connection. Knowing this means you should try to mix up your testimonials in any marketing piece you produce and have all types of people, including men and women of different races and occupations. Use full names and cities of origin if possible because people from the South still believe others from the South, and Northwesterners relate better to the people from their part of the country. You may not like this fact, but don't fight it because it's true.

RESOURCE: Check out www.CelebrityBrandingYou.com for our recommended resource for video testimonials.

Newsletters

We think a newsletter is one of the most important forms of communication you can have with the network of people you are trying to build. In today's high-impact media world, you have to always stay in touch with your network or they will forget about you. We aren't talking about just birthdays and Christmas either. We're talking about staying in touch with your clients at least once per month, and more often if you have good information. The easiest and most effective way to do this in the form of a newsletter.

The newsletter used most frequently today is an online version called an e-zine. We like e-zines and recommend them to all our clients. On the other hand, we strongly encourage using "snail mail" and sending your newsletter offline as well. This is one of your most important pieces of branding communication, but it is one clients resist because of the cost of printing and mailing it. *Please do not skip this important communication device.* People love to get something they like in the mail, and this has become more noticeable as the amount of mail you get today is not nearly as much as it was a few years ago, so it's easier to be spotted. Notice, we said people love getting something they like in the mail. Many people are tired of getting junk mail, but if they like what you're sending them, they start looking for it, and if the content is good, it becomes one of the first things they open. When you get to this stage in your client relationship, your connection has bonded.

In our business we have consistently published monthly mailed communications with our clients, from our own full-color, 82-page, high-gloss magazine on investing and wealth building to our multi-piece industry-specific newsletter, called *Celebrity Expert* Insider, that you can't get anywhere else. We also know many people use our publications as "bathroom reading," which most people don't do with the online edition we also send. Every once in a while, we're late getting the newsletter out—and invariably people call to let us know about it. They want the newsletter because it has material that's important to them, and that kind of relationship is exactly what you want to build with each of your customers.

Note that we said we send both the offline printed version as well as the online version of our newsletter. Like we said earlier, people process differently. We want to offer them information in alternative forms, so they can take it in the way they want.

6

Your Client Ladder Of Ascension

●6

Your Client Ladder Of Ascension

Your client *ladder of ascension* is the process that allows prospects to become involved with you on different levels with different fees attached. It is extremely important to understand that not all clients will have the same feeling about you and your service at the same time. You have to create different opportunities for them to be involved at different comfort levels. You only give a prospect the option of "yes" or "no" to work with your different levels, and let those who are not fully "sold" on your message work with you in a manner that fits their comfort zone.

In many ways, the client-development process is like dating. Seldom do you ask, "Will you marry me?" the first time you go out with someone. OK, sometimes it happens; they meet you and want every service you have to offer as soon as possible. Most, however, prefer to be courted. These prospects want to know that you really are who you appear to be, and that you aren't trying to hoodwink them the way so many others try to do. Today's prospects are often more skeptical than ever because they are constantly being bombarded with marketing messages. Fear of being taken advantage of is strong. Media clutter and fear must be overcome, and the best way to do that for most people is in baby steps.

To allow for the courting process, you must have a marketing lead-generation system to introduce clients to you and your product or service in steps. This system should give them opportunities to: 1) talk and relate to you, 2) buy a basic product or service that you have to offer (similar to going on the first date), 3) test your products to see if they do what you say, and 4) buy other products or services that you offer. Also like dating, the process can end quickly. To avoid this and continue to build the relationship, you must make sure that whatever your ladder of ascension looks like, you must make each and every person feel important, no matter what product or service they bought, whether it's the cheapest or the most expensive.

In a service business like ours, you should have several potential points of entry. The lowest on the ladder of ascension in our case would be to receive a free e-zine or article. The highest is the complete Celebrity Branding® Experience and would include a film on you and your business. Your ladder of client ascension might work like this:

- Free e-zine or free offer for a product/service.
- Purchase a book, or offer a selection of ones you recommend.
- Purchase an audio or video course.
- Attend a conference or special event you put on.
- Become a client for one product or service.

- Become a monthly client or private full-service client.
- Offer coaching or become a member of your mastermind group.
- Purchase an area exclusive license of your successful marketing services.

The accession ladder works because a client could contact you at any point in the process, and you would be happy to work with them. While, clearly, some of the levels are more profitable than others, you must treat all of your clients with the same level of courtesy and respect, because some of them may need to go through the process step-by-step.

Additionally, while some people who come into the ladder of services may not go all the way through the ascension process, they may refer someone who does. This is another reason you have entry options. A reader of our book might not want the Celebrity Branding® service but might think it perfect for their partner or a family member. If we didn't offer alternative services, that person may not understand enough about what we do for them to have the confidence to make a referral—and referrals are the life blood for service businesses.

The Dynamic Website: Your Keystone Branding Strategy

7

The Dynamic Website: Your Keystone Branding Strategy

The keystone in building is the stone on which the foundation and all the construction rests. Remove the keystone, and the foundation is unstable.

In today's business environment, the keystone is your website and internet strategy. Please note, we said two things—your website *and* internet strategy. Together we call these tools your Online Marketing Platform™. Indeed, having one without the other is futile. While putting up a website is helpful, you must understand what you want to get out of it. This is where most businesses fail. They believe having a website is all they need, and they're surprised when it doesn't generate the business they thought it would. It's like starting a new brick and mortar business, opening the doors, and expecting that's all you need to do... not the case.

THE ONLINE MARKETPLACE: THE FUTURE OF YOUR BUSINESS TODAY

Do you have any employees who work 24 hours a day, seven days a week, 365 days a year, can answer every question thrown at them, give prospects exactly the information they're looking for, collect credit cards, deliver products when a prospect is ready to buy, take down important questions from potential clients, and deliver them to you when you're ready to receive them?

We didn't think so. But the right kind of online presence can do exactly that, not to mention a whole slew of other things. But not just any website can accomplish these functions—what you must have is an Online Marketing Platform™.

If you don't have the right kind of website, you're losing out on an infinite amount of potential customers. It's kind of like sitting on the side of a river, with your rod lying on the ground next to you. If you don't put it in the water, you're never going to catch a fish. If your website doesn't have ways to attract prospects and get them thinking about your services, than you're missing a huge opportunity to build your business.

The purpose of this chapter is to open your eyes to what the *right* website can do for your business and how to go about building this powerful business tool that can go to work for you 24 hours a day, seven days a week, 365 days a year.

WHAT'S AN ONLINE MARKETING PLATFORM™?

An Online Marketing Platform™ (OMP) is a key element to your business because it features the right set of tools to attract prospects, give them just enough information to make them want more, and convinces them to leave you with their email address so you can contact them in order to turn them into a customer.

THE 16 SUCCESS ELEMENTS EVERY WEBSITE NEEDS

OMPs come in many shapes and sizes but have a consistent objective. They attract target prospects, project your brand, and capture the prospect as a potential client or customer. This is important because it's all about the customer. *Your objective is to capture the potential customer's contact information so you can market to them forever.* The customer is the real value of a business. However, until you get their name and contact information, you cannot establish a lasting relationship.

Following are the core elements of an OMP:

1. Easy, Clean Layout and Navigation
2. Newsletter Sign-up Form
3. Bonus Items
4. Blogs
5. Articles
6. Latest News
7. Testimonials
8. Contact Information
9. Calls to Action
10. Information About YOU and Your Business
11. Partner Links
12. Answers to Frequently Asked Questions
13. e-Commerce Capability
14. Social Media Links
15. Personality
16. Credibility

Let's discuss them one by one:

1. Easy, Clean Layout and Navigation

Don't overlook how important the design of your website is. In fact, as of March 2011, Google is now using actual human beings—a crazy concept, I know!—to rate sites for them. They're asking their raters to judge whether a website looks trustworthy, authoritative and professional, and whether it contains worthwhile and informative content.

We already know that Google hates squeeze pages because typically these one-page sites have very limited content and their sole purpose is to capture an email address, so many SEO experts speculate that they will slap sites that are overloaded with AdSense or flashy advertisements.

Now, more than ever, it is important for your site to look clean, professional, trustworthy—and have content!

Your navigation should also not be overlooked. Ever been to a site that just had too much going on, and you didn't know what to click on or where to go, so you just left the site? Sure, we all have! Don't make your navigation too confusing or have too many options. The old saying applies: Keep it simple!

2. Newsletter Sign-Up Form

If you aren't attempting to collect at least the email address of every potential client who comes to your website, then you're missing one of the greatest prospecting tools of our time.

Let's face it, the reality is that most people are too lazy to really figure out what they need, so they use today's most common research method, search engines, to try to find solutions to their problems. Odds are that even if you have exactly the solution they're looking for, they aren't going to be ready to hire you or buy your products the moment they land on your page.

Think about the way you browse the internet. If you're like the average surfer, you look at one site, then move onto another and so on until you either find the perfect solution quickly (which is rare), or you get distracted by something else and decide to come back later to find your solution. And when you sit back down to find your solution, how often do you end up at the same sites you stumbled upon the first couple of times you searched for solutions? Not many. *The businesses you visited before lost the opportunity to keep you.*

Why leave this to chance? What you need is a method of collecting the email address of every person who lands on your website. The easiest way to do this is with a newsletter sign-up form. It often looks like this:

Join Our Newsletter List and Get the Latest in Financial Trends!

Full Name:

Email:

CLICK HERE TO REGISTER NOW!

The purpose of capturing your clients' email addresses is to establish a means of contacting them. It would be nice to get all their information at this point, but it isn't going to happen. In fact, you're probably going to have to entice them with a benefit to even get their email address. A free newsletter is one way. Another way is to offer a special report, white paper, free trial or discount, in exchange for their email address.

This initial prospecting strategy allows you to use your website as a unique filtering device. As we have discussed, not everyone is immediately ready for your service. Potential prospects can visit your site, gather information about you, and mentally file it away for a future time when they need your service. Once you have their contact information, you can continue to market to them using a soft-sell, drip-marketing system that "automatically" stays in touch with prospects with a constant supply of information they want and need. While you're supplying valuable and interesting information to your prospects, you are also creating a database of future clients who are learning about you over time and are more likely to turn to you when they need your product or service in the future.

Because of this powerful contact system, your website should be devoted to creating extraordinary value for the people who visit. We are constantly amazed by the number of major corporations that "miss the boat" on their website and use it more as an institutional business card about their company. Bad thinking. *Use your website to be personal with everyone who visits.* Make the time that prospects spend on your site a valuable experience. Give them an opportunity to do some business with you, even if it's nothing more than giving you their name and email address in return for a special report or e-newsletter you offer.

3. Bonus Items

Everyone likes something for free. So give the people what they want! By using bonus items, you can get even more visitors to leave their email addresses with you. Some of the most commonly used bonus tactics are:

- Give visitors access to special reports that contain more detailed information than what's posted on your website. (A great headline can work wonders for getting people to take action.)
- Give away prizes. Who wouldn't sign up for a free iPad?*
- Give free tickets to teleseminars or live events on topics relevant to your target market.

*Make sure you check your state laws on drawings and giveaways. States usually require a few things in order not to cross the line into the world of "gambling" or "games of chance."

4. Blogs

Many of you know what a blog is, but for those who don't, it's a dedicated place for you to communicate with your customers and prospects. A blog (short for a web log) is an online journal or diary that allows you to write and post information or ideas you feel will be of interest to your readers.

How can your blog help you grow your business? Great question. To understand the answer you have to know a bit about how search engines work. Search engines like Google, Yahoo, Bing and all the others use what are called "spiders." Spiders are software programs that "crawl" the internet looking for new content and rank it based on its relevance to a certain topic. This is all done by some very complex math, but the important thing you need to know is that if you write frequently and/or discuss topics that are often searched online (for example, topics in the news), the search engines will consider your site "relevant." If you also include "keywords" (popular search terms) in your content that you know potential customers are searching for, there's a much better chance they will actually find you when they type those words in a search engine. The more often you blog using your keywords, the greater likelihood you will appear higher on a page when someone conducts a search using keywords related to your product or service.

Our three principles of blogging for search engines are:

1. Write Often
2. Write Relevant
3. Write Using Your Keywords

What Makes a Good Blog?

The only thing that really matters is the opinion of the audience you're trying to reach. Here are a few tips that will help you develop your blog to generate business.

1) **Know who you're writing for.** Is the market you're after boomer-aged adults, divorced men or women, businessmen or women on the rise? These are just the target markets for service professions we've discussed in this book; you know many other ways to break down your specialty. It's important for you to know who you're writing for so you can target your blog and other marketing materials to your specific target audience. The more focused you are, the more focused you'll be in the selection of your services.

2) **Keep it short and to the point.** Approximately 300 words—that's really all most people have the time to read for a blog. Remember, in the online world,

people are looking for actionable answers, not novels (or they would go to a bookstore). So keep your blogs short and to the point. Over time, this will build a great deal of credibility with your readers.

3) **Write actionable content.** "How-to's" and "Top 10" lists are great. It gives your readers action steps that they can take and use in their everyday lives. Think about ways to use this type of content to point out how you're different from your competitors. Remember to keep your specialty in mind as you write because they want this type of information. The more generic you are, the easier it will be for them to lose interest.

4) **Don't be afraid to tell some of your secrets.** People love to hear about how to make something happen, and then they love to pay someone else to do it. Let's be honest, even if someone just told us how to edit the code on our website to make it stick out like neon lights in a search engine, that doesn't mean we want to do it ourselves. All prospects really want is good, relevant content and then a way to contact you. After all, you just showed you're the expert.

5) **Allow comments.** Consider allowing people to post comments about your blogs. In fact, you should be the first one to post a comment after each blog. Pose a question or comment to simply get a discussion started. If visitors are interacting and writing comments about your blog, they're actually adding relevant content that the search engines are going to like.

5. Articles

A rticles work the same way as blogs in regard to driving up the relevancy of your website in search engines. The online game is content driven, so the more relevant content you have on a subject, the more likely you are to get traffic to your site. Articles allow you to show your expertise in a manner that's easily digestible to your visitors. The key to these articles—similar to blogs but slightly longer—is to keep them short and actionable. Give your potential clients information they can use, and they will trust you even more—getting you one step closer to earning their business.

Articles are usually a bit longer than blogs, but they don't have to be. Tell what you need to, but keep it slim. Remember, you are trying to build credibility as well, so try to keep your headline relevant to the context of your article. You should also keep your sales pitch to a minimum in your article. *There's nothing worse than looking for good information on a topic, getting three sentences into an article, and getting a blatant sales pitch.* Articles are meant to be informative, so try to leave the sales pitch out. At the end of your articles, consider adding a section like this:

> To get more information or to review other free special reports, visit www.CelebrityBrandingAgency.com. JW Dicks, Esq., Nick Nanton, Esq., and Lindsay Dicks, founders of Dicks+Nanton Celebrity Branding Agency® LLC, publish the *Celebrity Expert® Insider* a monthly newsletter covering topics that every person looking to build and brand their business needs to know. If you're ready to take your business to the next level, get more FREE info now at www.CelebrityBrandingAgency.com.

This type of informational offer is all you need to pitch a

prospect. Remember, we are always educating and offering good, relevant information on what our prospects want to know... By adding in a link to your website, if you publish the article on any other websites, you create additional inbound links to your site. This is another search engine optimizing key that helps bring traffic to your site.

In chapter 9, we'll show you how you can syndicate your articles to become an instant Celebrity Expert® and drive more targeted traffic to your website.

6. Latest News

This is an easy concept, but most people miss it: **People do not know what you are doing unless you tell them.**

It's as simple as that. Did you land a big contract? Did your business just celebrate its 20th anniversary? Are you under new management? Are you opening a new location? Are you involved in a charitable cause?

These are just a few of the questions that most of your clients would love to know. If they don't know, you simply aren't effectively communicating the answers. Having a "latest news" section on your website allows you to post such items in a manner that makes them look like news, not like you're bragging about yourself. Write in the third person for these posts, and they will really keep your clients in the loop.

TIP: When you announce news that involves other parties, mention them by name. Using other parties' names creates a doubly effective post because the search engines will now also pick up your site when surfers are looking for information about the other parties mentioned.

7. Testimonials

We already paid homage to testimonials in chapter 6, but in our opinion you can never talk about testimonials too much. Testimonials are amazingly powerful, yet often forgotten. There is no more powerful statement about your business than a third-party testimonial. Every person you do business with comes to you for a reason. Maybe you're the best at customer support, maybe you have the most convenient location, or maybe your venue is clean. Whatever the case, there's a reason.

You're missing a huge opportunity to learn more about your business and attract new clients if you don't ask your clients why they come to you. Ask your clients for the reasons, and they will give them to you. Have them write the reasons down or record them when they're talking, then you can use them on your website (and everything else) to help convince new clients that other people love doing business with you, so they probably will, too. Oh, and there's no such thing as too many testimonials!

Think about it, if you walk into a business and see hundreds of thank you letters from clients posted all over the walls, you're going to ask yourself one question, "What have I been missing?" Because if all of those people are happy enough to write letters, then you're probably in the right place.

Testimonials can be in many forms. The best format is video, just behind that is recorded audio with a photo, and last, but definitely still miles ahead of having nothing, are written testimonials with or without a photo. The internet is a mixed medium, so take your pick!

You have to be conscious of making sure your testimonials

don't look manufactured and that they're believable. The best way to do this is to give specifics about the individuals who give you testimonials. Here is a common format for doing so:

"Testimonial Here..."—First and Last Name, Title, Company or Organization, City, State, www.Website.com.

8. Contact Information

You MUST make it easy for visitors to reach you and ask for more information. Make sure you have at least a phone number (800 numbers are best) and an email address on every page. Studies show that putting these at the top of your website, on the far right, is most effective.

You will also find that some visitors want to type a question to you and don't really know-how to use email well, so don't miss out on getting the business of these folks, too. You can cater to these visitors by creating a web form that they can fill out and submit to you without needing to use email. Here's a common format for a "contact us" form:

Name: [   ]
Email: [   ]
Phone Number: [   ]
Comments/Questions: [   ]

CLICK HERE TO SUBMIT!

Tie all of the forms you have on your website to your database system, because some people will email you a question and never sign up for your mailing list. You don't want to forget about these people or lose their information, so add them to your database automatically.

9. Calls to Action

Ever been to a website where you weren't sure what the company did and had no clue where to go once you got there? Unfortunately, that's true for a lot of the websites we see out there. Most people who come to your website don't know exactly what they should do, so you have to tell them. You can do this by using what's commonly known in the marketing world as a "call to action."

Here are a few examples of calls to action:

- Click here for a free white paper on the 10 changes to the new tax law that will affect your business!
- To get our newsletter sent to you free every month, sign up here now!
- For a no-obligation appointment to discuss your situation, click here!

You get the picture, but the key is to have compelling headlines that will make your visitors take action now! If you want them to buy something, tell them. If you give them a good reason to do what you say, most people will usually listen.

10. Information About YOU and Your Business

One of the biggest fears for most people who are thinking about doing business with you online is that they don't know you personally, and they want to make sure you aren't trying to scam them. The best way to remove this fear from site visitors is to literally take it back to elementary basics, as in "show and tell." By this I mean you should both show *and* tell visitors who you are.

Tell them about your company:

a. When it was founded
b. Where you are located
c. Who the principals are
d. Who the core management team is
e. Who some of your customers are
f. What you do

Show them pictures of:

a. Big events you've attended (trade shows, symposiums, seminars)
b. Your office
c. Your products
d. Key executives
e. Recreational activities and events with clients and staff members

These are just a few examples. Remember to treat them as if they were walking into your office for the first time. What do you have in your lobby that tells clients who you are? What about in your office? Do you have pictures on your desk? Do you have diplomas on the wall?

Although, internet visitors can't have the same experience they would if they walked into your office to meet with you, there are still ways to create that feeling. One great way is with video. You can film a video tour of you and your office, and walk the viewer through what they would see and encounter if they were to walk through the doors of your office, including "meeting" the key people in your office. They will absorb information about you visually as they see your office and the pictures and awards you have hanging on the walls. All these scenes, used properly, convey positive information about you and let the prospect in a little on who you are and whether you're the person they want to work with.

Remember, don't try and appeal to everyone. The more you do that, the more you will appeal to no one. Try and be who you are. The people who are attracted to that are exactly the type of people you want, and these people are the ones who will be with you for a long time. Make sure they know that you're a real person and that will clear a huge hurdle in getting business in the online world.

One of my favorite quotes, *"Be who you are and say what you feel, because though who mind won't matter and those who matter don't mind." –Dr. Seuss*

11. Partner Links

We all use search engines to make our online quests easier. The reason being is because they're good at what they do, and we've come to know and to trust the results of the search engines.

In order to keep the search engines working and to keep their customers happy, search engine companies do a lot of work behind the scenes to make sure the results they deliver are valuable and accurate. To do so, they use complex mathematical equations called algorithms. Although these algorithms aren't published publicly anywhere, for SEO, (search engine optimization) the two most important elements of the search engines' algorithm are keywords and backlinks.

Backlinks are links that lead back to your site from other sites. The higher the relevancy of that incoming link to your website, the greater value it has to your site. So search engine spiders scour the internet to see how many sites link back to yours. *The assumption is the more people who link to your site, the more valuable your information is.* Of course, there's one caveat: The links have to quality ones.

Search engines are not stupid, so don't even think about using the trick of posting your site on "link farms," spammy sites you can pay to link back to your site. Instead of helping you, these can actually hurt your ranking.

What you're looking for in a link partner are quality websites that have something to do with the business you're in. Then try to get them to link back to you. How do you do this?

We've found the easiest way is to offer to trade links. All you have to do is look for websites that are the most respected in your industry and email the webmaster to ask if they'd like to swap links. You will agree to post a link to their site, if they will post a link to yours. Once they agree, just post it on a page on your website that features all of your "preferred partners," which is really just a nice page with lots of links to other sites.

If you'd like to try a more advanced strategy, type a keyword into Google that you would like your site to have a high ranking for, and look at the first page of results. Copy and paste the domain names of the sites on the first page of Google's search results. Then for each of the domains you listed, type in Google's search bar:

Link: www.InsertDomainNameHere.com

This will allow you to see what other websites are linking to each of the sites listed on the first search page. Then you can email those sites and ask them if they would be interested in swapping links with you. This one simple tip can get you a lot of traffic and a much higher page rank.

12. Answers to Frequently Asked Questions (Objections)

In the world of sales, we all have to deal with "objections." Simply put, objections are reasons people might not do business with you.

Here are a few common objections:

1. Price is too high/low
2. Quality isn't good enough
3. Location is too far away

As you might have guessed, there are countless other objections. Often the reason consumers don't buy products and services is that they make up their own answers to questions because no one is there to answer them, especially online!

What can you do to avoid this? Beat them to the punch: Provide answers to these questions and others that your customers often ask. To do this, we create a "Frequently Asked Questions" page (an FAQ page as it is known in the online world), and we list the common questions our clients have along with the answers.

This strategy isn't used nearly enough in the online or in the offline world. Just a few simple questions and answers can remove a lot of fear from a potential buyer and move them one step closer to becoming a client.

When someone signs up for your mailing list, don't assume they've read all the content on your site. A great strategy is to email your list of FAQs to the potential client. You can email them one at a time or email the entire list. We've found that this can greatly increase your response rate!

13. E-Commerce Capability

Every year, consumers are getting more comfortable buying online. Your site should give them that opportunity. It's not always a great fit for every business, but if it makes sense for your website, go for it! After all, it's one of the only ways to make money while you sleep. We can assure you that the first time you wake up and find unexpected funds in your bank account, you'll have a big smile on your face...trust us!

14. Social Media Links

Today, social media is a *must*. It's not only becoming more and more important because search engines are using it in their algorithms, but it's social proof for your business. Consumers are now looking to their "friends" on the various social media sites for advice and solutions to their problems. Because of this, you need to make it as easy as possible for visitors to not only see that you are active on the social media sites but also to share your content online with their "friends." The best way to do this is to encourage visitors by linking your website to your social media sites. We suggest doing this by putting the logos of each of the sites that you are active in on the top of your site or sidebar, and linking the logo to your specific account. Make sure you also put a CTA (or call to action) by the logos that says "connect with us" or "share our stuff."

15. Personality

You've heard us say it before, "People buy people." This philosophy should be no different on your website. Gone are the days that you can throw up a website, and it's enough to get you business (if there *really* ever were those days). Today, people are business—and they're going to do business with people they know, like and trust. Your personality and *who you are* needs to shine through on your website. *You* are the first step to someone doing business with you.

How do you do this?

Here are some ways you can display your personality on your website:

- Video
- Pictures—not only of you and your team but also of your family on your "About" page
- Audio
- Your Blog

Remember; let your personality shine through. In the end, it's what connects you to your buyer.

16. Credibility

Credibility is another key element on your website. Nobody knows you're the expert unless you tell them—and your website is a critical place to show this.

People today are skeptical; showcasing your credibility is one of the ways to cut through any doubts. If you have been in any media outlet, make sure you display that somewhere prominently on your website. If you haven't been in any media outlets yet, don't worry; there are a lot of ways to gain credibility on the internet, even without this exposure. Becoming a part of trusted companies like the Better Business Bureau and the National Ethics Bureau, and displaying their logos on your site is one of the many ways you can increase credibility.

WHAT TYPE OF WEBSITE DO YOU NEED?

This question confuses people who don't understand that there are many different types of websites with different purposes. Most people only have one website. Unfortunately, having only one website reduces your opportunity to present your story to different people in different ways. Not using the right type of website to convey your story is also a waste of time.

Clearly, everyone needs a main website as the hub of their business. You should also consider an additional site for each target market you serve, or even each product or service that you offer. By having more than one website, people can access and get the specific information they need instantly, without being confused by things that aren't relevant to their needs. While at any of your sites, you can always take the opportunity to lead them to your main site where they can get more information about your expanded array of products or services.

We discussed blogs earlier in this chapter. You can make your blog part of your site, but you can also leave it to stand on its own (i.e., allow visitors to access it at the domain www. YOURSITEHEREblog.com). This is another example of the power in multiple sites. People who find your blog through your promotional efforts get instant gratification of what they were looking for, and, based on your blog's design, you can let them know there is more information available on your main site and have a quick link that takes them there.

There are many other ways to use multiple websites to increase your exposure. Think about having a dedicated website with a sales letter for each product or service you offer. It's a great thought, isn't it? And…yes, it works!

To start, concentrate on your main site. When it's completed, remember to be open to new opportunities to expand on the web.

8

Your Online Marketing Platform™: Design, Build, Promote, Monitor And Optimize

8

Your Online Marketing Platform™: Design, Build, Promote, Monitor And Optimize

N ow that you know what makes a great website, let's talk about a few more important steps: how to get a website built, promote it, and use it to create revenue.

PHASE I: DESIGN AND BUILD

Construction

M uch like building a house, there are many decisions to make when building your website. To keep the analogy rolling, in many cases you can act as the general contractor and hire subcontractors to do the heavy lifting, or hire someone to be the general contractor for you, and they can handle everything.

If you hire an individual or a firm to handle everything, make sure you create a list of deliverables and time limits for completion. Look at samples of past work to see if you like their finished product. Never pay all the money for the project upfront, and tie compensation to performance, especially when it comes to meeting deadlines.

If you are brave enough to oversee the entire process, and just subcontract with others to get the job done, here are some practical tips we've learned that will save you some time, money and headaches.

Planning...or Lack Thereof

The first step in having a website built is to plan for what you think you are going to need. Gather samples of other sites that you like so you can see how they are laid out, the style of design you like, what some of the best sites are doing right, and what some of the worst sites are doing wrong.

Once you've done this, you can start creating a content outline. Start by numbering a piece of paper and writing down your key web pages, the ones that will be the hubs of your site. For example you might have:

1. About Us
2. Testimonials
3. Contact Us

You get the idea. As you continue, you can break down each page to show what will be included on it. Here's another example:

1. About Us
   a. Picture of key personnel
   b. Two to three testimonials

      c. Paragraph about what you do

      d. Links to three of your best-selling products

Continue to do this for the rest of the site. Once you have a good outline, you can start to get some idea of what this site is going to cost. Without the outline, no designer can give you a realistic quote because all websites are not created equal! Which leads us to our next point...

All Web Designers Are Not Created Equal!

There are many factors to take into account when hiring a web designer. We hate to be stereotypical, but web designers can be very artsy, very techy or both. When you get web designers to quote your project, pay attention to how they treat you. If they're exceptionally hard to get in contact with, think about how you'll feel when they have a significant amount of your money as a deposit and you still can't get a hold of them, or when they're a week late on your deadline, and you can't get them to return your calls.

If a designer treats you in a way that you aren't happy with before you even give them any of your hard-earned money—*run*. This is a bad sign!

A good web designer should be professional, have a good eye for art, and should be able to advise you on the smartest way to build your website for it to accomplish your goals. Don't let them talk you out of what you want! Many designers are horrible businesspeople and will try to put form over function. Remember, you're the one who knows your business. Don't let a designer try to pitch you on something that you know won't work. If it doesn't work for you in the offline world, there's a great chance it won't work for you in the online world.

One great place to find web designers is Elance www.elance. com. It's kind of like an eBay for subcontractors, except that you post a job, freelancers bid on it, then you choose the designer you want to work with and award them the job. Once again, use common sense, check their portfolio, check their feedback from previous customers, and always use Elance's payment method (because it protects you from indiscriminate people who are just trying to take advantage of you). There are many other places where you can find good web designers, not the least of which is a referral from someone who you know who has a website that works (meaning it generates business). Another site that has given us great results is www.craigslist.com. Just remember, don't throw your common sense out the window!

Considerations When Having Your Site Designed

Design

Your design should be in keeping with your brand and should be an extension of your company in the offline world. Prepare a list of parameters for your designer that outlines the colors you're willing to use as well as colors you hate. Describe your ideal customer and include samples of sites you do and don't like. This will give your designer a good starting point.

Navigation

While many people don't think much about how visitors are going to get around their site, this can be a fatal flaw in converting visitors to clients. While animation and drop-down menus look neat, remember that not all web browsing software programs are created equal. This means there will be users who do not have the latest technology and thus may not be able to view your high-tech menu. While getting fancy can be fun, you want to make sure that a visitor never has to "figure out" how to browse your site. If they have to think too hard, they will likely just leave your site for one that isn't so hard to use.

Look at some of the biggest moneymaking sites online: Amazon, Ebay, Google. Notice that they are all extremely easy to navigate. There's a reason for this!

Search Engine Optimization (SEO) Considerations

Three tips that will make you look like a web pro and keep your web designer on his toes!

While we could write a series of books on SEO alone, and many of the advanced strategies are beyond the scope of this book, a little knowledge in this field goes a long way. SEO is one of your key online marketing tools. As a matter of fact, here's a great test for any web designer you're thinking about hiring. Ask them their thoughts on "SEO." If they fumble, or worse yet don't even know what you're talking about... *run!*

The way your site is designed can help or hurt the way your site is viewed by search engines. Here are just a few SEO rules you need to make sure your designer adheres to:

1. Use text as often as possible.

Here are several uniform fonts that all web browsers can display. If you use a font outside this realm, your designer will have to create an image using the fancy font, and it will display as an image on your website. The problem here is that search engines cannot read images, and this will put your site at a disadvantage for online marketing.

2. When you do use images, use alt tags.

A picture is worth a thousand words. Don't think that we're discouraging the use of images. We use them on all of our sites. When you use an image, there's a tool called an "alt tag" (or image tag) that allows you to describe the image. Make sure you use these; it's like giving the search engines a helping hand to decipher what's on your site. The more you try to help search engines, the more relevancy they will give your site, and the better your ranking will be.

3. Give each web page within your site a different title.

Tell the search engines what each page is about by giving each page a unique title that contains the main keywords and phrases that address what's contained on the page. Putting keywords (but not too many!) within the title of your pages is a great SEO technique that will help your website climb up the rankings. It will also allow your visitors to remember exactly what your page is all about when they bookmark your site or save it to their "favorites."

PHASE II: PROMOTING YOUR WEBSITE

5 Traffic-Generating Tips That Will Have Potential Clients Beating Down Your Virtual Door

The majority of websites fail because they only complete Phase I. They build a website believing that people will now beat a path to their door. Unfortunately, this isn't the case. If you've ever had a website, you probably know what we mean. Your site must now be promoted in order to get the results you want. The more it's promoted, the more "hits" you get. The more hits you get, the more interest that's generated in the site from all sources—individuals to search engines. Creating a buzz about you or your business is the most important phase because without it everything you did in Phase I is wasted.

I. Keywords

Keywords are what your clients are looking for. If they're looking for anti-aging medicine, their keywords might be: anti-aging, feel younger, look younger, young again, etc. If you don't know what your clients are looking for, this is a question you need to answer because it's the foundation for promoting your site.

To get an idea of what your clients are looking for, use Google's keyword tool at: https://adwords.google.com/select/KeywordToolExternal. All you have to do is type in several of the names of your products or services, and it will give you suggestions.

Another great tool is Wordtracker, www.wordtracker.com. Wordtracker can help you see how many times a particular word is searched. It actually gives you a rating you can use to see if you should spend time trying to promote a keyword, or if you should look for something else because the market for that word is too cluttered.

Using these tools, you can take a look at what your clients might be typing and then find the best combinations of words that will attract new clients. Similar to fishing in a river with the wrong bait, the wrong keywords can lead to a dry harvest.

2. Pay-Per-Click (PPC) Advertising

Pay per click is considered by many to be one of the most effective forms of advertising because you pay only for people who come to your site from the ad you place. The keywords we mentioned above are often great pay-per-click words as well, but there are many more that you can also test.

Popular search engines like Google and Yahoo/Bing use pay-per-click ads for their top results on their search pages. Quite often, the pay-per-click ads are placed at the top of the search page and down the right side.

The way it works is through an auction system. The words that are in highest demand, command the highest prices. The amount you bid determines your placement on the search pages. You want to try to make sure you show up on at least the first page of the search because most people never even get to the second page of search results.

Most search engines that sell pay-per-click words will allow you to set a bid for the keywords you are interested in and a daily budget that you don't want to go over. There's only one way to see what works—test, test, and test some more. Don't be afraid to spend some money here, but monitor your spending. We can't tell you how many horror stories we've heard of both novice and experienced pay-per-click advertisers who've blown more money than you'd like to know on keywords that didn't work. Don't do this to yourself until you fully understand the process! Start with low limits and adjust them as you go. For the most part, web traffic follows patterns. So don't worry about getting all of the traffic today. In all but the most unusual of circumstances, we can assure you it will be there tomorrow!

3. Blog Syndication

We talked about blogs earlier in the book, but one of the best tools for promoting your business and your celebrity-expert status is to syndicate your blog. You can use many tools to do this, but one of the easiest is www.feedburner.com.

What happens when you syndicate your blog is that you turn it into what's called an RSS (Really Simple Syndication) feed that users can plug into their RSS reader. This way, they can keep the newest content that you write flowing through their RSS reader without constantly having to come back to your site on a daily basis (which most people simply aren't willing to do). It takes some work to gain this sort of trust from your readers, so don't be discouraged if getting RSS subscribers doesn't happen overnight.

If you don't have an RSS reader, we recommend www.iGoogle. com. It allows you to organize all kinds of information, including RSS feeds. It's like having all your favorite newspapers in front of you at one time, and you can keep them up-to-date without having to visit a bunch of websites. Try it out, and then you'll understand why syndicating your blog is so important. It makes it very easy for those who want to keep up with your latest posts.

4. Feeder Sites

As you are well-aware by now, one of the key strategies in creating your celebrity-expert status is creating actionable content that your clients can read. We advocate doing this in the form of blogs and articles. You can post both to your site, and, as discussed previously, you can syndicate your blogs. Now, we're going to tell you how you can syndicate your articles too.

Until recently, "article marketing" was a great way to distribute your content online. However, with Google's ever changing algorithm, article marketing (sites like submityourarticle.com and ezinearticle.com) no longer carries the SEO weight they once did. Although, if you have your content posted on these types of sites it won't negatively affect your rankings, it just doesn't really help you. So with that being said, the best way to distribute your articles online now are with what are called "feeder sites."

Feeder sites allow you to post your content on a specific niche for free. Basically, you're creating a mini website of articles all on your specific topic and either throughout the post or at the end of the article they have a link back to your website.

Sites like Squidoo.com and Knol.Google.com (yes, this one is owned by Google) are great examples of feeder sites.

5. Online PR and Press Releases

No one knows what you're up to if you don't tell them. While this sounds like a ridiculously obvious statement in your personal life, most businesses don't adhere to such common sense.

So how do you do this? Press releases are one of our favorite ways. You can write them relatively easily yourself or hire someone to write them for you.

Now, we'll let you in on a big secret: All the official-sounding press releases that talk about a company winning an award or doing something great are written by or under the supervision of the company that the press release is about. It's almost as great as a testimonial because it is written in the third person and sounds like news, not like you are bragging.

Once you write a press release, you should post it in a "latest news" section of your website. While this is a great first step, the next step is to syndicate the press release.

Make sure that when you distribute the press release online, at the end of every release add a section that explains who your company is and what you do. This is another great place to put a link to your website. When you syndicate the release, it will create inbound links to your site, which, as we discussed, are great for boosting your ranking in the search engines. Here's a sample format you can use:

About Dicks + Nanton Celebrity Branding Agency® LLC: Dicks+Nanton Celebrity Branding Agency® LLC celebrity brands entrepreneurs and professionals as experts in their field of business and helps them expand nationwide. JW Dicks, Esq., Nick Nanton, Esq., and Lindsay Dicks focus on helping their clients grow their businesses by gaining media credibility, using specific proprietary systems. For more information, visit www.CelebrityBranding Agency.com.

Here are a few great sites you can use to syndicate your press releases:

1. www.prlog.org: free but very effective

2. www.prweb.com: offers several levels of service to choose from and even provides podcasting and search engine optimization

3. www.pitchengine.com: similar to prweb (but much cheaper!)

Give it a shot. You'll be pleased to see how quickly your news gets picked up!

PHASE III: MONITOR, OPTIMIZE, AND CREATE NEW REVENUE STREAMS

Marketing is a moving target. Just like building a website (Phase I) and not promoting it (Phase II) is a bad idea, Phase III is equally important. The best part is, once you're aware of how the online world works, this is where you'll discover a treasure trove of untapped markets. As you delve deeper into your online business to determine what works and what doesn't, you'll find market niches that aren't being served. When you discover these markets, you can quickly reposition to serve that market with just a few tweaks of your current marketing, promotion and pay-per-click strategy.

This is ultimately what Phase III is, the opportunity to optimize your business and create new revenue streams.

What Works?

Some people believe they know in advance what will work. But while we all try to make the best educated guess we can, ultimately, until you test something, everything is just that—an educated guess. The market is ever changing, and "what works" is a constantly moving target. This is the ongoing phase of your online business. It definitely takes some work, but without it you can quickly find yourself spending marketing money in the wrong places, and believe us, it goes quickly!

Monitoring and Reporting

As mentioned previously, you absolutely must monitor your online efforts in order to quickly shuffle your marketing efforts, and dollars, out of campaigns that aren't working and into campaigns that are generating income.

To monitor your traffic, there are many tools you can use; however, as usual, Google has given us some free tools, so we advocate using those!

1. Google Analytics (www.google.com/analytics)

This can be installed from your Google AdWords account, or, if you don't have one, go to the website above. All you have to do is enter your site information, and it will spit out a line of code. Give this code to your web designer, and Google Analytics will start tracking what happens on your website. It does more than we could possibly hope to explain to you in this book, but what we can tell you is that digging into the functionality of this software is very worthwhile, and extremely helpful in determining where traffic is coming from, and why the traffic is or is not hanging around long enough to convert into customers.

2. Google Alerts (www.google.com/alerts)

Did we mention we love Google?! Google has given us all another free tool that allows us to stay up-to-date with where information about you is coming from and where it's posted.

What happens is that you can type any word into Google Alerts, and then, when Google indexes a new web page that contains the term(s), it alerts you.

Some great uses for Google Alerts are:

1. Tracking where your press releases are posted

2. Tracking where your articles are posted

3. Monitoring your competitors
4. Monitoring your industry

5. Keeping tabs on who's talking about you on their blog or website

There are an infinite number of other great uses as well; all you have to do is use your imagination!

We use both of these tools to monitor our own results and the results of our clients.

9

Promoting Yourself
Offline

9

Promoting Yourself Offline

Today, more than ever, we are increasingly wooed into thinking that business is only done on and through the internet—from Amazon.com and the iTunes Store, to the continual growth in e-commerce, Facebook and other social media platforms, and even the cost effectiveness and precision of email and pay-per click marketing.

It would be easy to rely simply on the internet to create your brand and promote the products and services you offer. And while the power and the potential of using the internet to increase your revenue is very real, it is also constantly changing and adapting and is truly only one media channel with which to share your message.

The Direct Marketing Association (DMA) shared that marketers and businesses spent more than $50 billion on direct mail alone in 2011. They also went on to share that for every $1 spent on direct marketing and advertising in 2011 resulted in $12.03 of incremental revenue across all industries.

In this chapter, we're going to discuss the six fundamental aspects for building a client base through your Celebrity Branding® and increasing your cash flow using offline and direct marketing strategies that we have used to build our own business, and used in the successful marketing of our clients around the world. We call these six steps the Celebrity Expert® Marketing System.

While you might think many of these strategies seem obvious, the beauty of them is exactly that—they're obvious, but not many businesses take the time to execute them. And we can promise you one thing, if you implement these strategies, you'll definitely stick out over and above the crowd of your competitors.

6 STEPS FOR INCREASING PROFITABILITY AND DOMINATING YOUR COMPETITION

Step 1: Identify the True DNA of Your Business and Marketing

The first step toward any winning marketing system through Celebrity Branding® is to assess, plan and strategize around who you want to do business with, and how you are currently marketing to finding your ideal client or customer.

You will want to work with your team to determine:

- What is the profile of your buyer?
- Where are they coming from?
- How are they hearing about you?
- What are they buying?
- What makes them an ideal client?
- Who isn't buying?

- What makes them an unattractive prospect?
- Who else are they buying from?

After you have answered these questions, it's time to look at your current marketing channels, advertisements, media outlets, copy, media and content, and determine if it is effectively working to help you find and attract more of the clients you have determined were best to work with.

Determining your client's true DNA and the DNA of your internal marketing and advertising messages lays the foundation for which the next five steps are built upon.

Step 2: Craft Your Core Message

In today's marketplace, Celebrity Branding® is all about telling stories. Traditional marketing, branding and advertising tells facts, features and analysis. To get the attention of the market that we established in the first step, you need to tell stories that have an emotional tie to your audience. From car dealers to tax attorneys, there is a story behind every business.

In this second core component, you need to create and position your "Core Story" to the marketplace. In this story, your goal is to connect the dots that take "what you do," whether you are a doctor, real estate agent, author or sales professional, to who you are as a person and what you stand for. Once you combine these factors, you will have a winning strategy to attract and keep the attention of your market.

Once you craft your story, you need to create media pieces and vehicles for others to hear and relate to your story. One of the best ways to do this is through a book.

Imagine having your clients beg to spend eight, nine or more hours with you to listen to you tell them what your business philosophy is and how you can help them. This is exactly what you get to do with a book! The amount of time that you can get inside the head of your potential clients is endless, especially when you tell your story.

Most people think it is difficult and expensive to publish a book or that you have to get a major publishing deal, but this couldn't be further from the truth. You can self-publish your book by having it printed by a printing company that specializes in books. You can find many such companies online by searching on your favorite search engine. One of our favorite options is CreateSpace. CreateSpace is owned by Amazon.com and offers all the services you need to publish your book. When you're done, they will even sell it on Amazon.com for you!

As the demand for writing and publishing a book has increased for our clients, we have developed a publishing company of our own and helped over 900 authors become Bestselling Authors over the past three years. These authors include those who write an entire book themselves to authors who write one chapter of a book with other authors. These books are called compilation books. This is a great way to get started as a writer and bestselling author. For more information on our book publishing process, please visit www.celebritypresspublishing.com.

Another valuable place to share your core story is through audio and video. From CDs and MP3s to podcasts, audio is one of the best ways for clients to not only get access to hear your story but also hear the power and emotion in your voice. A great way to start recording audio is to use a free software program from Audacity and purchasing a USB microphone from your local electronics store. Using these two elements, you can easily talk right into your computer, recording your story and then saving it as a file to share with clients and prospects.

These audio files can then be transcribed into special reports, manifestos or briefings that tell your story in another way.

A third way to share your Core Story is through video. Whether you are shooting a full feature documentary about your business, or using a Flip Camera to share your message, using direct-to-camera video is a great way for your marketplace to see you, your personality and your passion for what you do. Sharing these videos online through YouTube and Vimeo or through DVDs that you mail out or give away to prospects is a great way to show off your Celebrity Branding® Power!

A true Celebrity Expert® uses multiple formats of media to share their story. Begin to explore with telling your Core Story through different mediums and then using that story in all of your marketing efforts.

Step 3: Set Up a Lead Capture and Database Management System

Every step in the Celebrity Expert® Marketing System builds upon each other, and in this step, we combine the marketing data and research from step 1, along with the Core Story creation in step 2 to drive new and interested leads through a lead-generation system designed to highlight the benefits of your business and convert these prospects into paying customers.

You are going to start by developing a lead-capture page,

commonly referred to as an opt-in or squeeze page, designed to collect the names and email addresses of inquiring online traffic. The sole purpose of these pages is to collect this information in exchange for something of value that will help the prospect in their quest for information to solve the problem they are having.

In addition to lead-capture pages, you can build your database through 24-hour free recorded messages. These messages tell part of your story and offer a free report, CD or other type of media created in step 2 in exchange for the prospect leaving information at the end of the message.

The great thing about the lead-capture page and the recorded message is that they work to grow your business and your database 24/7/365 and can be used in conjunction with all your advertising and marketing efforts. From phone numbers in the Yellow Pages or in direct mail postcards, to sales letters or magazine ads, your call to action and value proposition allow your prospect to get exactly what they want without the feeling that they are being sold to or pushed into a decision.

Once you collect these leads in your new lead system, you should immediately place them into a follow-up sequence in the attempt to further solve your prospects' problems through your products and services.

A common way to address this is through an e-mail auto responder sequence where you have pre-written messages loaded into an e-mail service, such as www.Aweber.com, www.1ShoppingCart.com or www.InfusionSoft.com. Services such as these will send your pre-written e-mail messages to your prospects every day, on time, and help them to make an informed decision and take action to use your product or service.

The same auto responder technique can be applied to direct mail as well. From sending automated postcard mailings to a three-step letter sequence, you can work with your local printer to create an automated mail campaign for all of your new prospects that leave their address on the free recorded messages.

These types of auto campaigns should be setup to run for at least 30 days from the day they signed up to inform the prospect of services, benefits, case studies and action steps. Once you set up a good follow-up system, it can run for you day and night to bring in leads.

Part 4: Give Your Leads Something to Be Excited About

Celebrity Experts® do not just send links or tri-fold brochures to qualified prospects; they send a "thump" that lands on the doorstep of a potential client. From building kits and putting together boxes with movies, DVD's, CDs, books, newsletters, client case studies, promotional items and more, you can literally shock and awe your market till the point where it just isn't fair any more.

When you have a qualified prospect who meets the criteria we established in Step 1, someone who is primed to do business with you and become a great client, it is your responsibility to impress them, show that you are the expert and someone they need to do business with.

Start by sending them a *Shock and Awe package* in the mail. Nothing gets someone's attention like a package arriving at their door. To take this to the next level, would be to FedEx a package overnight. Before your competition has time to get to the post office to buy stamps, you will arrive in style, get past the gatekeepers, and deliver your message and your value right to the person in charge when they are still fresh and thinking about you and how you can solve their current problem.

To do this, start by collecting all the media items that tell your story: all your press clippings, client testimonials, or other materials and promotional items, and find a box they all fit into. Include a welcome letter that explains the items, what you want them to do with the items, and what you want them do to next (*hint: it's to sign up to do business with you!*).

You will also want to develop and create a monthly, print newsletter that you send out to all your current clients and to your warm prospects. A newsletter is really just a collection of your information presented in any fashion you want. The key factor to realize here is that this is a way to stay at the top of your clients' minds. *With a newsletter, they will receive whatever information you want to give them at whatever time intervals you choose to give it to them.*

You can fill your newsletter with the latest information in your industry that will make your clients take action and call you. For instance, if you're a mortgage broker and interest rates are at an all time low, wouldn't it be great to write a short article about how this can affect monthly payments and remind your clients that you can help them lower their payments because of the new rates? The possibilities are endless, and this works in every industry!

We've seen everyone, from doctors, accountants, carpet cleaners, mortgage brokers, real estate agents, local restaurants and just about every business in between, use the newsletter strategy to drive business. Your newsletter can be as long or as short as you'd like. You can include success stories from past clients, congratulations to clients who have used your product or service successfully to change their life, coupons for discounts on a featured product or service, and much more.

A newsletter is essentially a way for you to speak to all your clients and prospects every month, to let them know how you can help them, just like you've been helping others. We have created and written newsletters for over 25 years in every business and industry we have ventured into. And the result is the same thing every time…more business, more referrals and more opportunities to share a little bit of you and your company with the people that allow you to be in business in the first place.

Part 5: Treat Your New Clients Like Celebrities

Your marketing truly begins when a client begins their professional relationship with you and as such, you need to begin treating them in a way that amazes them at every turn, as if they were now playing the role of Celebrity.

From the minute they come on board with your business, you want to send them a Welcome Kit that includes a letter from the owner, or CEO, welcoming them to the program and to your business, detailing the experience and what to expect next and throughout their relationship working with you. You should also include the CD of your Core Story, a signed copy of any books you have written, or media pieces that helps them solidify their mindset that you are the right person for the job. Hopefully you are starting to see a trend here!

Make sure to truly take care of your customers and clients and get these Welcome Kits out as soon as possible. You never want your new clients to feel like they are waiting for something to happen. Usher them in with great confidence.

On top of the welcome kits, you want your new and existing clients to feel appreciated. Develop a Holiday system to do just that. From birthday cards, to holidays, thank you gift cards or a box of cookies to bring in the season, you want to create a plan to keep your clients thinking about you with attention-grabbing campaigns throughout the year.

Begin to think about the holidays that you care about and celebrate and involve your clients as well. From wearing silly Uncle Sam hats and sending out July 4th postcards to Thanksgiving letters letting your clients know that you thank them for working with you, holidays are a great time to bring everyone together.

During the on-board period of working with a client, you also want to develop this type of relationship. Using a similar strategy to Step 3, you can automate postcards to go out 30 days, 90 days or 1 year into your working relationship to inform them about progress, things they should be experiencing, or asking them for feedback to improve their experience.

No matter your business, you need to treat your clients like Celebrities, rolling out the Red Carpet for them whenever you can. After all, they are the ones that keep your lights on and food on the table, right?

Part 6: Invite Your Clients Into Your Life

Once you have developed a great first impression and welcomed your new clients into your business family, you want to continue to keep that impression lasting for the lifetime of the customer. The best way to do this is to continually update your clients and customers about your life, your business and the things you are doing to help change the lives of your clients and customers. At this point, you should be mailing newsletters out on a monthly basis, but now it's time to take it up a notch and create a business that will continue to impact customers over generations.

You can accomplish this by taking this newfound relationship with your clients and allow it to grow your business by telling people all the things you do. One of the three profit multiplies of any business is to get your existing clients and customers to buy more of your products and services. Thus, you need to start Step 6 with a catalog.

Why more businesses don't have a catalog, I do not know! Think about your existing customers, how many of them actually know about all of the things your business offers. If they knew about more of your services, do you think they might buy more of them? Of course!

Even service-based businesses should have a catalog. From sharing stories about the different types of law that you practice to breaking down circumstances, types of cases and stories of your evolution as a business, a catalog is a great place to use images, words and color to show your clients you are more than a one-trick pony and you can help them in so many more ways

And now that you are providing a valuable service, shocking your clients and keeping their attention every month, it is time to develop your referral program. Here is the thing about most referral programs, if you do not have one, you do not get referrals...

If you do not ask, you shall not receive, so it's time to start asking. Designing a referral program can be as easy as asking for a referral and creating a reward system for the referrals. Start by looking at different interactions and emotional states that your clients have when working with you. Where are they the most excited and emotional when doing business with you?

It is at this point that you should ask for a referral. You can send a postcard or a letter that arrives in their mail around this time, or you can generate a phone call to ask about their experience and record or write it down.

The reasons referrals work so well is that the person who is doing the referring already knows, likes and trusts you. They like your work and are champions for the services that you offer. When people love a product or service, they tend to tell others. Your job is to make their telling of your story as easy and seamless as possible.

Once you create a consistent and systematized referral program, your business will begin to grow organically with the right kind of client already pre-sold on how you can help them. It is then up to you to put these new clients through the six steps above and create a winning cycle for your Celebrity Brand!

These are six very powerful steps that we use in the offline world and in our own marketing; your imagination will help you find many, many more. The key to remember when using the offline Celebrity Expert® Marketing strategies is that many of your competitors have simply gotten too cheap and too lazy to creatively market and go through the steps outlined above. If you implement even some of these strategies, you'll set yourself apart from your competitors and further solidify your Celebrity Expert® status in the minds of your target market.

For more information on the Celebrity Expert® Marketing System and how you can personally work with us to become the Celebrity Expert® in your area, contact us at info@

dnagency.com. We look forward to hearing from you and helping you change your business to become everything you want it to be.

STAGE 4

Rollout: Expanding Your Celebrity Brand Business

10

Capitalize And Roll Out
Your Celebrity Brand

10

Capitalize And Roll Out Your Celebrity Brand

Congratulations! You now see the process of "Celebrity Branding You®," and you understand the potential it holds for you to expand your business and eliminate your competition. We now want to expose you to the "next level" of Celebrity Branding®. We will show you how to capitalize on what you've accomplished to deliver the kind of money you always wanted to make.

At this point of the Celebrity Branding® process, you've built a good name for yourself in your area of expertise, at least on a local level. You've created methods to bring in prospects and convert them to customers. You've written a book or at least special reports in your field expertise. You may have started speaking to local groups or created your own seminar program. Whatever you've done, you've created a process to brand yourself as the expert in your field.

The next level of income stream for you is to create a business on top of your existing business by becoming a consultant or coach to others in your field who don't compete in your geographical area.

The branding process you've now created can be packaged and duplicated all over the country by different people who are in your same business, service or profession. You do this by creating a marketing package for your system, then selling the total the package along with training or coaching to other people in your field for a substantial fee.

If the concept of creating a system for your business and a national expansion of it doesn't immediately click for you, think in terms of a franchise. By their very nature, successful franchises are centered on a proven system of operation and then expanded throughout the country to individuals who believe in the system and wish to execute it in their local market.

Your proven system of operation, combined with an offer of an area exclusive to a local person in another area operating that system, is similar to how a franchise works. However, some people like this system better than the franchise because they keep their own name and run their own business, answering only to themselves, but have your experience to help guide them in areas like marketing where they may not be as strong as they are in their actual profession. While not all the experts who do this national rollout add the area-exclusive element, doing so tends to increase the value of what you have to offer because the buyer of your services is more comfortable knowing you won't be showing someone else in the area all your secrets.

While this next level of business growth can be a little intimidating until you learn the ropes, the millions of dollars you can generate from it will make learning the process all worthwhile. Yes, we said *millions of dollars*. While we don't want you to think of this as a get-rich-quick program, we do want to encourage you to believe in the possibilities and think of it as a wealth-building system for you and your family because there are many people doing it and in all types of industries. In fact, the entire process is also like a trade association where common businesses come together to learn industry best practices.

Let us give you some examples.

- *Dan Kennedy*: Dan is certainly one of the premiere marketing coaches in the country. He has a library of products and services to get you involved with him and his organization, and once you're part of it, it's very difficult to leave. The reason it's so hard to leave is because what he teaches and what he sells rings true. Once you find someone who's good at what they do when you need what they have to offer, you become very loyal. You can visit Dan's site at dankennedy.com.

  As you look at Dan's products and services, note how carefully he relies on giving you irresistible offers backed by long guarantees. He does everything he can to get you involved, but if what you buy is not right for you he makes it easy for you to get your money back. The reason for this approach is he does not want to hassle with people who don't want to follow his methodology or waste time. A quick sale is not the point. He's trying to build a valuable lifetime customer. Of course, this is an important lesson in itself.

  As you look at Dan's websites, you will also note that

he uses numerous levels of customer participation to take you through the processes of ascending through various levels of working with him and GKIC, the organization marketing his services. You start with a Gold Level service, offering newsletters and other info products, all the way up to private-level coaching at $27,000 per year, or Private Client consulting and copywriting services with even higher fees attached.

- *Jay Kinder and Michael Reese:* Mike and Jay are in the real estate business. They became so successful at creating specific systems to follow to get property listings and sell them, even during the recession, that agents from all over began clamoring for their training. To meet the demand, they started a teaching course and then added high-end mastermind and coaching secessions that helped other agents learn their proprietary processes. The demand for their help became so strong that Jay and Mike formed their own real estate association, The National Association of Expert Advisors™, to begin specialized training on how to be a different type of real estate agent and to transform yourself from salesman to Expert Advisor™.

- *Matt Zagulla:* Matt is a financial planner in a small town in West Virginia, and yet he is one of the most successful experts at what he does in the country. As an expert, he began to differentiate himself from a person who just sold financial products to a financial advisor who built a practice centered on building trust with his clients first.

As the expert in his industry, Matt began to teach

other financial planners around the country his methodology and how to connect and create a bond with customers based on trust. His expertise in this process helped him build a new successful business based on his processes, and he now coaches other financial planners all over the country on building their practice using his marketing and client relations program.

- *Ben Glass*: Ben is an attorney in Northern Virginia. He actively practices personal injury law but also has a large family that keeps him active as well.

Ben became known as an expert by his peers in the legal profession on how to advertise in a heavily regulated environment and how to attract new clients in a very crowded legal field. Not only has Ben continued to grow his own law practice, but he now helps attorneys all over the country grow and market their practice in an ethical way in various legal specialties.

- *Sean Greely*: Sean is a leader in the fitness industry. He has literally shown thousands of fitness professionals how to grow their business way beyond what they thought possible by using marketing and sound business processes to bring in more clients and also run their business more effectively to make and produce more income in the process.

Because of his success, Sean has expanded his business and holds major events each year to train other trainers and fitness leaders, along with advanced marketing practices that bring in more business. He has transformed his fitness business to a larger one of education and marketing for other fitness professionals.

These are but a few examples of successful entrepreneurs and clients of ours, who have taken their local success in their field, Celebrity Branded themselves as the Go-To Expert, and gone national. *They've taken an ordinary business and made it extraordinary.* The businesses that have followed this model are diverse, including restaurant operators, carpet cleaners, foreclosure experts, dentists, chiropractors, vegetarians, insurance agents, and dental schools. The point being, any business can make this type of transformation—and, best of all, the financial results are extremely lucrative for those who succeed and take their business to this "next level."

AREA-EXCLUSIVE LICENSE

There are several ways to structure your system for national rollout. A moment ago we alluded to the well-known franchise concept. The advantage to the franchise concept is the fact that it's just that—well known. When you speak to people about owning a franchise, they've heard of that type of operating business system, so you don't have to explain the concept. Instead, you can focus your time and energy on selling the franchise itself.

However, the problem with a franchise system is that it's expensive to launch, and many people just don't want to risk a fairly large amount of money on something they believe will work but may not have the full confidence to back their belief with money. Others simply don't have the money to invest.

The Area-Exclusive License (AEL) is a solution to the financial dilemma. An AEL is structured to have many of the same benefits as the franchise, without all the regulatory costs normally associated with it. We've spent a great deal of time and money in our law firm carefully structuring the AEL to be exempt from the franchise rules and business opportunity laws. Additionally, we monitor the laws for changes and adapt the AEL agreements to them.

The key to being successful in these types of programs is to provide full disclosure to your clients of what you can and will provide them so they don't think you have overpromised. As we've said before, please understand that this type of a program is not a get-rich-quick method. These programs, like franchises, are processes and systems used successfully and then expanded to other areas. None of the experts are trying to make a quick sale or taking all buyers who want in. There are screening processes to find clients who are right for the business, and the experts are in their business for the long term.

HOW THE AEL WORKS

The Area Exclusive License, despite our own spin on it, isn't a very new concept. In fact, large companies and big celebrities such as the NFL, NBA, Disney, Universal Studios, Dan Marino, Wolfgang Puck, and every college in America use some sort of variation of a license agreement to let others use their name for a fee. Some of the companies and celebrities combine the standard product license and an exclusive territory to create an entity structure similar to our AEL. You can now experience similar success by licensing out your own proven business process. Let us walk you through an example.

Assume for a moment that you're in the real estate business. You've created a specialty for yourself working with investors. You've chosen this area of specialty because unlike the residential sales market, you aren't as affected by a down market and have investors who like to buy in all kinds of situations. Investors are always buying real estate in good times or bad because there are different reasons to purchase real estate in different economies. For example, if the market is overbuilt and sales are down, this is precisely the time to look for bargains in foreclosures. If the market is strong, you may be looking for real estate that has development potential or strong cash flow. The point is, there's always a market for investors.

If you were this real estate person, you could follow our four-step process for Celebrity Branding® this expertise, with you as the Celebrity Expert®.

Step 1: Build Your Expert Status

First, you would brand yourself as the Celebrity Expert® in the real estate investment field. In doing so, you would create your "ladder of ascension" for people to first learn about you, buy small educational products where you teach your concepts, and then buy more products and services as they see what you say works and you develop a closer relationship with them.

One way this process has been successfully done is to sponsor local lunches where the investors could come hear you or your guest talk about the real estate market. The first lunch would be free and then you could charge the investors to come to more training.

Normally you only break even profit-wise on this first level of education because you want the investor to get to know you and identify you as the expert in this field. So to increase attendance, you hold the cost down for the investor. Building relationships in a rush is not the best way to build trust for the long term.

After the investors have participated in the lunches, they are offered an opportunity to move up your ladder of ascension and get in on the inside of investments in your area. This next level could be paid training or a service you provided.

Following this next level of service, you can add on higher levels of coaching or offer to work with the client as his exclusive "buyer's broker." This agreement promises you that if they buy any real estate, they will buy from you and no one else in exchange for the work and education you're providing. In some cases, programs like this offer an even higher service, and, of course, higher fee for the investor ($250 to $500 per month) who want to get "first look" at any of the properties you find. In this example, you're getting paid some impressive numbers from these investors just to be part of your inner circle. These fees can be on top of your commissions or credited against any commissions you earn. Either way you're getting monthly income streams, even if you don't sell anything that month.

Step 2: Create Your Online Marketing Platform™

As we described in chapter 7, your Online Marketing Platform™ will provide a continuous flow of leads and build your celebrity status in potential investors; eyes by providing a stream of quality content in your specialty. Will every person who gets your content become a client. No. But that is fine because the do-it-yourself person is not who you are looking for. Those people can go out on their own. You're looking for the person who's interested more in your expertise than they are in doing it themselves. When you find these people, they will typically translate to long-term clients and bring their friends to work with you as well. This is your perfect scenario.

Step 3: Implement Your Offline Marketing and Development Strategies

Your offline marketing accomplishes the same as your online branding, except it reaches different types of people looking for information from different sources. Refer to chapter 9 for a refresher course if needed.

Step 4: Package Your Area-Exclusive License and Sell It to Other Realtors

This now brings our Realtor example up to speed. You've built your online, offline, marketing and business development system. You know what direct mail works to get people to your lunches. You know what type of speakers you should have as guests. You've designed a buyer's broker contract you know works and as legal teeth to it. All these concepts are a part of your system to work with real estate investors. Now you package this system and offer it outside your area to Realtors in other cities who would like to work with investors like you but don't know how. Your system is the answer.

Congratulations! You've just built a new business on the back of the successful one you already had.

Question? How much would you pay someone who had a proven system like the one we just described if you were in the real estate business? Remember, in exchange for your investment, the value you get is a marketing and operational system that's proven to work—and all you have to do is follow it.

The answer? People are paying between $15,000 and $40,000 per area exclusive territory. Think about it: How many areas of exclusive territories do you have to offer? Just for fun, let's say 400. Additionally, we'll assume the upfront fee for an area is $20,000. What's the sell-out value to you? $8 million.

While $8 million is nothing to sneeze at, here is where the real interest will kick in for you. All these programs also have a residual or continuity fee that goes with them. There are some very high ones, but typically, they range from $487 per month to $1,000 per month. The residual fee is for continued support, coaching and ongoing new marketing ideas that you will provide your licensees. Now for the math: Assume you're able to do 400 exclusive areas times the low range of fees ($487). This gives you a monthly residual income of $194, 800. Annually that's $2.3 million. Exciting, don't you think?

What if you can't sell 400 territories? Instead, you can only sell 100. In this case, at $487 per month, it still provides you with a residual each month of $48,870. In addition, don't forget you still have your original local group you started with, plus the upfront fees on the 100 areas you sold. Impressive, don't you agree?

We think that the AEL is truly one of the most exciting ways to build a successful business in the country today. Remember, our example was only for real estate, but there are all types of industries doing this: doctors, lawyers, mortgage brokers, carpet cleaners, financial planners, online business gurus, health trainers, you name it. If you have a successful business and can brand yourself as a Celebrity Expert®, can teach others how to do what you did, this is a powerful way to build a legacy business.

And you know what? We're not done. There's more in the final chapter for you to learn!

STAGE 5

Selling Your Business And Creating "Legacy Dollars"

11

Develop An Exit Plan

Develop An Exit Plan

We hope you're energized with excitement and that your brain is rushed with great ideas for your business and what you can do with it.

In some respects this final chapter dampers the enthusiasm of building and running a successful business because we talk about selling it. Nevertheless, an exit plan is always important for a business because it's the ultimate capitalization.

Once you've completed your Area Exclusive License process, you have the unique product of a business income stream that can be monetized. The process can be done in several ways.

1. Sell the income payment to the licensee for a prepaid discount.

2. Sell the income stream to a buyer/investor.

3. Combine the AEL in a city or state and sell off that part of your business to an investor to take over.

4. Roll up all the licensees into one large company and

sell to an institutional buyer. (This gives the licensees an opportunity to monetize their value as well.)

5. Roll up the entire group of licensees as suggested in #4 but also add their real estate companies to the sale, creating a larger sale.

6. Roll up all of licensees and their real estate companies into a single company and take the company public through an IPO.

While a detailed discussion all these exit strategies are beyond the scope of this book, we throw them out quickly because they're exciting to think about and let your brain work on them as possibilities. In many cases, the final roll-ups are into franchise systems because they ultimately provide more control to you as the founder and a greater exit plan for all. Roll-ups can, however, be done just as AELs, and we think we will see that soon. In fact, we hope to be able to report the roll-up is YOURS!

12

The Final Chapter– What's Next?

12

The Final Chapter– What's Next?

A s of the writing this book, many of the strategies we have outlined are cutting edge, but we all know things change and we must find "the next big thing."

Just as those of you who are successful in life and in business know that you can't expect to stay at the top of your industry if you relax once you reach the pinnacle of success, we also know that you will need to stay on top of your "Celebrity Banding" process. In order to make this easy for you, we've created free updates and special reports you can sign up for at www. DNAgency.com. These free tools will help you keep up with all the newest tips and strategies that we uncover as we continue to work with some of the biggest and best in the business.

Be sure to visit the home page of www.DNAgency.com to sign up for our free CelebrityZine™ as well as to find many great resources you can use so you won't be left behind. We look forward to hearing about your success and welcome your correspondence.

Here's to bringing out the Celebrity in You!

BONUS SECTION
Special Reports For Growing Your Business Today

13

Top 10 Ways To Grow Your Business Fast

Top 10 Ways To Grow Your Business Fast

Unlike some of the David Letterman top 10 lists, which give you a list of items in reverse order of their importance, each one of the 10 ways to grow your business fast is important. The most important is the one you think your business can implement quickly and efficiently. That strategy will differ depending on where you are in the growth cycle and what you may have already implemented in the past.

As you read the list, you will see some strategies you might be familiar with but haven't implemented because you didn't think they applied to your business. Try not to just skip over the strategy, but consider it a moment in your present circumstance, which may have changed such that revisiting the idea may now be fruitful.

Another interesting way to view the list is not just with an eye on your own business, but on the business of others you may come in contact with. Few people have ever stopped to think about working on other people's businesses like we do every day. However, we suggest that you might consider this growth opportunity for yourself. Some of you have become successful at executing one or several of these strategies. So successful, that the knowledge becomes a growth strategy for you in and of itself. The reason is because you now have the ability to help others "see" the opportunity and collect a fee for advising them, or take it as step further, and help them implement the growth strategy in their business. You work on the business strategy with them in a joint-venture capacity.

Good ideas for business growth are a dime a dozen. Having the knowledge and ability to implement them is a key element to success. With that said, let's look at the strategies.

1. Joint Ventures (JV) and Affiliate Agreements (AA)

While joint ventures are nothing new to the business world, their use is accelerated through the web and e-commerce. Offers of creating affiliate agreements (AA) are commonplace in the wired world in particular, and many of these relationships develop over time into the more formal arrangement of a JV.

From a terminology standpoint, AAs are less formal and may be a precursor to a formal JV. While AAs are created on the fly (quickly formed and often quickly dissolved), JVs take more time, structure and documentation. This is not required legally, but it is the way people think of their structure.

Both AAs and JVs are formed for many reasons, but here are some examples:

- **Joint promotion of products or creation of a special event**

- Developing a new product or service
- Developing a new market, such as an international expansion
- Developing or sharing new technology
- Creating common distribution channels
- Pooling resources of capital, intellectual property, employees or physical property

All these types of inter-company relationships have been formed as either AAs or JVs, and all have been both successes and failures. The problem, of course, is not the structure, but the people or entities behind the structure that make or break the deal. Some people aren't cut out to deal well with others in a business relationship any more than some people are unable to get beyond their own objectives to see that the relationship works for both parties. Because of the potential problems that can come up in either of these business structures, a simple rule develops. The more money that's at stake, the more care and attention should be placed on formally structuring a legal relationship that doesn't risk either party's current business.

We have used AAs and JVs as a major marketing channel for building our business. While they often take time to arrange and build a trusting relationship between the parties, once the connections are made, they can last for years with both sides profiting from the arrangement. We highly encourage and recommend their use to build your business at any stage.

2. Licensing

Licensing has become big business today and is a great money generator because, in most cases, it is an extension of what your business does, as opposed to being the product or service that drives the train. There are exceptions to this generalization, of course, and there are even large companies that focus only on buying products or businesses that can be licensed.

The reason licenses are so profitable is that the cost of developing the licensed goods or services has already been spent, and the license agreement is now sold on the basis of a percent of gross sales. This means that the licensor has no responsibility for ongoing overhead or other worries affecting the traditional bottom line aspects of the business.

The law around licensing is that you transfer to another part certain "rights" to the product or service as opposed to ownership. These rights can be broad use, or they can be structured with limited use and restrictions. The structure of the license requires great balance. The more restrictive you are in granting the license, the more control you have and the greater value of your remaining license rights as the licensor. On the other hand, if you are too restrictive so that the licensee cannot make money, you as the licensor won't either, and your opportunity to sell more will decline.

When people think of licensing, they often think of character licensing, such as Winnie the Pooh, Mickey Mouse and Spiderman. Additionally, sports organizations, such as the NFL, NBA and NASCAR have extremely successful licensing divisions. On the other side of the business spectrum, there is considerable licensing in software, biotechnology and telecom. These are all examples of the big-business licensing producing millions of dollars for the licensor and huge opportunities for the licensee.

While big businesses profit from licensing, so can small businesses, and you should keep your eye out for opportunities. Strong databases are frequently opportunities available for licensing or "renting" for businesses that have done a good job of documenting their customers and collecting email and home addresses. These lists of buyers are very valuable to other businesses that might have a complementary product. Offering license right to the other businesses gives them the opportunity to have additional prospects that would otherwise cost them more money than they're spending for your license. The license you agree to may be a one-time use, or it may be continuous. Additionally, the license may develop into a larger strategic alliance or JV if the licensee is a success.

Licensing can also play an important role in the growth of young companies, and used this way, it can be a form of expansion capital. For example, your young company may not have the cash to expand into the international market with a product that has been successful in the U.S. Instead of waiting to have the expansion capital and losing time, you could license the right to promote your product overseas to one or more licensees who promise to put up money and promote the product in new marketplaces. Yes, you may give up some of the potential profits that you might have made if you pulled it off yourself, but the current license fees and the first mover advantage you get by acting now could far outweigh the "potential" you might lose.

3. Growth Through E-Commerce

Every business should have a web presence. Unfortunately, many companies have websites that are outdated or that are little more than a business card on a computer. This is a very bad business strategy. Almost the first thing people do at the beginning of a business relationship is to check you and your company out on the web. What they see determines in a large part their perception of you and whether they will do business with you.

Websites and the strategy of effective e-commerce are a

necessity for a company looking to grow. Your e-commerce plan must be one of capturing potential customers and moving them into the buying process instead of standing around waiting for someone to find you and hope they stumble on your contact information. Why wait for a customer to find you when you can go find a customer? This is the essence of having a real e-commerce strategy that separates successful businesses in the offline world.

Ask yourself an important question: What is your e-commerce strategy? Does it have its own plan of business operation, or is it just a supplement to your current business plan without any regard for it's own budget and financial plans. Why miss the additional revenue offered through the online world?

While we think you should take advantage of each opportunity and strategy you have available, you may not always have the time or resources. This is when you begin combining some of the 10 strategies in this chapter. In this case, if you can't afford to, or do not know how to take advantage of e-commerce, consider spinning that part of your business into an entirely different company with its own budget. You might even consider funding this part of your business through an investor. Leave the e-commerce application to someone who's a specialist in the online world, and let them create enhanced opportunities that you're missing today. The new mantra of today is to open your business and let others create advantages you don't have the resources to pull off.

Another opportunity to consider, if you are short on time or money for an e-commerce presence, is to consider licensing your e-commerce intellectual property to someone who is an expert in the field. Since you may never reach your potential for an e-commerce strategy on your own, joint venture it with someone for a percentage of the business.

4. Ideas and Concepts

Generally speaking, an idea or concept does not qualify for a patent, copyright, trade secret or trademark protection. You will lose the potential economic benefit of the idea or concept if you voluntarily disclose it, unless you can satisfy three rules:

1. The idea is in concrete form.

2. The idea is useful and original.

3. The idea is disclosed in a situation where a business relationship is planned and compensation paid.

While meeting this test is not always easy to prove, the use of a non-disclosure agreement (NDA) and a non-circumvention agreement will help you prove elements of the test have been met. On the other hand, these agreements can also be an impediment to getting an opportunity to make a presentation. Many large companies are taking the position that they will not sign an NDA because would-be investors are using contracts so broad that other potential opportunities could later be brought into the web of inclusion.

If you have a good idea, you should definitely try to profit from it. Creating specialized NDAs that are very specific may get you past the gatekeepers, or sometimes you may just decide to take the risk and let the deal out, then memorialize the discussion you had with the other party, in writing, to demonstrate proof of disclosure. Neither is a perfect approach, but it's the cost of doing business; sometimes you won't get compensated when you think you should.

Concepts that you already use in your business are a little

easier to protect. This may be everything from a new way of marketing a product to developing a distribution procedure that has not been used before. One way to capitalize on this information is through the consulting format. This strategy can be very lucrative for the consultant who truly has information that can help someone save a great deal of time and money when implemented.

Some other examples of non-tangible ideas or concepts:

- Inventing and exploiting new products or services
- Opening new distribution channels
- New production and training techniques
- New promotional marketing campaigns
- Establishing new pricing methods or pricing structures

5. Real Estate Opportunities

Few companies view real estate as a corporate growth vehicle until it hits them in the head. McDonald's is a classic example. After opening thousands of stores in prime locations all across the country, it discovered it had amassed and held billions of dollars worth of real estate. It's not alone either. Other franchises learned from McDonald's discovery and are capitalizing by selling off their real estate assets to public real estate companies, some of which they had a hand in forming. These franchises not only make money on the initial sale, but they also collect ongoing property management fees and sometimes a percentage of growth of the asset. By looking at a traditional business expense differently, they turned it into an asset with huge economic added value.

Smaller companies have also experienced growth through real estate by using their office needs as a way to buy real estate. Yes, the Great Recession put a damper on appreciation, but interest rates are low and opportunities are out there.

Strategic use of your own company's needs can also leverage you into bigger properties. For example, in our current economy, most banks require pre-leasing on new construction. A company can develop a piece of property that is bigger than its own needs and make money on the sale of the additional property. An alternative, if you aren't an experienced developer, would be to joint venture the property with a developer who gets a fee for his work, but you make the spread between construction cost and the new value after development.

6. Mergers and Acquisitions (M&A)

M&A is always an exciting item of business news, as billions of dollars change hands with each merger or acquisition. However, these are usually just the headliners. Smaller, but perhaps just as important, transactions occur where local businesses buy competitors or complementary businesses. For example, a printer can either grow by increasing its marketing efforts or by acquiring other print shops. By acquiring other shops, the buyer can make money immediately on the acquisition spread or by synergistic savings when the companies merge. The benefits from these mergers or acquisitions come from many possibilities, including staff reduction, price increases because competition is eliminated, and leveraged intangible assets, such as cross selling to a new database that one company had but the other didn't.

Mergers and acquisitions require more specialized knowledge to make sure you are not being taken advantage of, but your first acquisition is typically a learning experience. Future acquisitions become more formulaic, based on how the first was structured and modified as adjustments were needed.

Growth through mergers and acquisitions can also have a second advantage. Not only can you profit from the immediate synergy but as a company becomes larger, it also becomes a more interesting acquisition prospect to even larger companies that are willing to pay higher multiples. This means a possible increase in profit potential just on the arbitrage factor of smaller company value vs. larger.

7. Franchise

Other than e-commerce, franchise growth opportunities may be one of the biggest for you and your company. There are several layers of potential: One is the opportunity to create your own franchise that grows into a huge number of stores, and two is the opportunity to buy into someone else's franchise in the early stage and get a master franchise for a strong territory. This could come about by spotting a successful West Coast franchise just starting to spread its wings and locking in the right to the South, or even just a big state like Florida. People have made small fortunes getting in on the ground floor of new franchise opportunities, but you do have to investigate both the strength of the concept and the management team you will be working with.

Another less-traditional opportunity comes from buying a successful franchise and adding it to your existing non-competing but complimentary business. For example, a printing company might add a sign franchise and to it's existing storefront location. The two companies would experience a cost savings from doubling up on space and employees, while cross selling to each other's customers with different needs. This move would add a whole new line of products with less incremental costs attached. The local print shop might benefit from the national name and exposure, and the franchise could benefit from the print business's local reputation.

8. Intellectual Property

Intellectual property (IP) of all types is another way of growing a business. Patents, trademarks and copyrights on products or materials can be licensed, franchised, spun off or sold to produce additional revenue for a business.

Even names themselves have become highly marketable. Key domain names sell for millions, but even smaller names can be sold for five- and six-figures. We have sold this type of IP for clients and even ourselves. Once you train yourself to see the opportunity, bundle the domain name in a package that includes a functioning website or a trademark. Do that extra IP work, and you have an even more valuable commodity to sell.

We encourage our clients to regularly take an IP audit of what they have that could sell to someone who might be interested in building a business around it.

Simply trademarking great names that you own or use can be a terrific part-time job opportunity.

9. International Expansion

Clearly, the world is getting smaller, and ventures are taking place all over between people who never dreamed they would be doing business together because of previous geological constraints. Now, all businesses have an opportunity to expand internationally either through e-commerce, by using the web to find contacts and sources that can help overseas. When seeking distribution channels for your product, it's a lot easier to find people and contacts through the web as opposed to having to go overseas and starting blindly. Additionally, other countries want to take advantage of American products and know-how. Entrepreneurs in these countries seek out Americans with products and services to introduce to their country and marketplace. People may not like America's politics, but they like Americans, and they like the opportunities they can have working with American businesses.

If you have products or services you think would do well internationally, join some of the respected international chambers of commerce that can help you get connected in a country for a small investment in their membership. The reverse is equally true if you want to import products from abroad. Seek out information about who to do business with from a specific country's trade organization or chamber of commerce.

10. Consulting and Coaching

In the past, people who started consulting businesses have had a stigma of not being able to do anything on their own, so they defaulted to the field of consulting or coaching. While this can still be true, consulting has turned around into big business again as everyone from Bill Clinton to Donald Trump is willing to lend their name, expertise or connections in exchange for a fee.

Consulting or coaching is a great way to monetize your intellectual property power that you have created in your business or profession. Additionally, consulting and training are huge time savers. It is often said it is not the things you know that kill you in a business endeavor, but the things you do not know. Using someone with experience who can guide you along the growth path at a faster and safer clip can be worth its weight in gold. This fact is particularly true in this fast-paced world, where someone else might be creating the same idea you are, right now, and it is a race to the market with the first one there winning all the chips. Don't shortchange yourself. Learn to spend money to make money, particularly if it can be at a faster pace with a leveraged return multiple times that of your initial investment.

If you are successful or have a unique knowledge base, consider offering your expertise to others who you could help slash the learning curve and save them money or make them more. As long as you can show the potential clients a good return on investment, they should be quick to take you up on the opportunity.

In summary, each of the 10 strategies mentioned can be a powerful addition to your business growth plans. Most companies never get beyond the implementation of a few, so by the addition of even one more to your arsenal, it can make a dramatic impact on the bottom line.

14

8 Power Principles To Make More Money While Working Less

14

8 Power Principles To Make More Money While Working Less

By Nick Nanton

The idea of working less while making more is a daydream that society has been enjoying for decades, but as time goes by we seem to be doing just the opposite. The idea of taking control of our lives sounds like a "pie-in-sky" scheme, but if you follow my structure of how life should be, your productivity and bank account will increase and your stress level will decrease. I have developed eight power principles to help you generate more money and free time while working less in today's 21st century work environment.

The 1st Power Principle: Developing the System

If any business is going to be efficiently operated, proper management of time and money is imperative. Methods of doing less and earning more are concepts we've all thought about, but most of us probably haven't given it much credence. Frankly, from childhood we are groomed to work hard. It is in our nature to get up in the morning and prepare for a hard day's work. But if we're honest with ourselves, sometimes we get off track and become too focused on the job and little else. We all need to stop and enjoy life now and then. People in business today need to learn to develop systems that will help save time and effort.

When you create systems for your work, you'll find that you can grow your business exponentially. When we start a small business, we normally have to do everything ourselves. What we need to learn to do is take our "secret sauce" that we've developed and turn it into a system so that anyone can follow the formula, either a whole plan or in pieces.

Many entrepreneurs just don't feel comfortable sharing their personal workload—that is the problem. They either feel guilty or they are too frugal, and they continue to try to do everything themselves. I'm a lawyer, so I'll give a legal example because lawyers are actually pretty good at this, but only because it has become customary. We create a system for what we do well, or likely what can only be done by a lawyer, and then we can turn over the non-legal portions of the business—the research segments—to someone else. The lawyer can then review the findings, analyze the results, make the decisions, and then spit out a legal action plan for what needs to happen or draft the necessary contract. With a system like this, you can use your "highest and best use of time" by creating a system that allows someone to step in and help you complete your workload so you can do more of the work you get paid more for and less of the work that either doesn't have enough value, you aren't very good at or you simply don't like doing.

Another habit that can be dangerous to an entrepreneur is the mentality of "I'm the only one who can do this particular task the right way." They want to get their hands dirty, and sometimes these unique businesspeople are very possessive about their businesses. This is quite often the biggest hurdle to the issue of creating systems and outsourcing projects to other people. You have to focus on doing the things that you do well, but you need to create a step-by-step guide of how you need to do things in your business. Take the time to consider the various tasks that keep your business running, and write out a step-by-step system so anyone could walk in and accomplish the end goal with little direction. Having a system will help you in the event that someone has a life-altering incident that prevents them from coming to work for six months. By having a system, you guarantee the job will continue to be accomplished no matter who shows up for work on any particular day. It will really take a lot of burden off of the business owner. Then, all you have to do is monitor the system while accomplishing the tasks that are more relevant and, more important, make you the most money.

The 2nd Power Principle: The Importance of Scalability

If you can create a scalable system to assist you in running your business, you will be able to exponentially grow your profits as well. Scalability is the concept of doing the same amount of work while reaping greater rewards. Most people are excited when they hear that. Let's use the example of a business coach. If I'm a business coach, I can teach you over the phone, one on one, or I could set up a teleconference where I could teach 1,000 people the same concept at the same time. So I would be doing the same amount of work in the form of teaching a concept, but instead of sharing the information with just one person, a teleconference could expand my reach without taking any more of my time. Essentially, the main concept of scalability is that it is possible to sell 1,000 people into the conference, and while it may cost you a few extra cents per person, you're doing the same amount of work while getting paid by 1,000 people versus just one. That's powerful.

The 3rd Power Principle: Outsourcing

This principle is a concept that many of today's Fortune 500 companies have already embraced, but it is still one that most small businesses may not have even considered. We see in the news almost every week that companies are shedding personnel in order to get "lean and mean" and more profitable.

The old way of doing business is to hire a bunch of people, bring them into the office, and make them sit at their desks and do their jobs (or more likely surf the internet all day and not do their jobs). Think about what you are doing, as the business owner, when you create this obsolete business structure. You wake up at the same time each morning, eat the same breakfast, and travel the same route to work; you've just created your own rat race. Rather than using this method of doing business, we advocate taking advantage of technology. We have access to every communication medium imaginable: teleconferencing, video conferencing, email, instant messaging, online message boards, cell phones and wireless email devices like BlackBerrys and iPhones.

Using today's technology, you don't need to be surrounded, in person, by a bunch of capital-intensive employees. You can have 99 percent of the task performed by an outsourced person off-site that you could have executed by someone who sits in your office, draining your resources each and every day, whether you have something productive for them to do or not. In today's market, you can outsource anywhere at any time, whether it's to a friend or a neighbor looking to make a few extra bucks or someone overseas. The best part is you usually don't have to pay a fixed monthly fee for their equipment or their overhead; you are only paying for the service they provide to your business when you need it. You pay a little more on an hourly basis than you would for someone working full time in your office, but you are only paying for the service when you need it. If the workload is slow, they aren't sitting in a cubicle, chewing gum or surfing the web and exhausting your limited resources.

Another positive side is that this kind of business structure also allows you more freedom because you don't have to be in your office at the same time every day to make sure your employees are doing what they are supposed to be doing. You do have to be organized, because you have to be very specific with your wants and needs, which usually forces you to write a detailed plan for the task. Then you must determine how much you are willing to pay for the task to be completed. You can outsource the job to someone who is willing to do it. There are some great places to find people you can outsource work to. One of my favorites is called Elance (www.elance.com), a site for freelancers. You can post a job on their site for just about anything, and then other people bid on the job. Much like eBay, there is a feedback system. You can pay through their system with deposits, and they escrow the money until you approve its release. I think everyone should try it out sometime. It may not work for you, but it's worth a shot! Oh, and just remember, the cheapest provider is probably not the one you actually want to hire. In many cases, you really do get what you pay for. Another popular service that specializes in overseas labor is www.YourManInIndia.com.

The 4th Power Principle: Positioning Yourself in the Marketplace

Setting up a process so a budding customer base can find out who you are, what you do, and how to contact you is crucial if you expect to nuture and expand your business. In order to move forward, you can't be apprehensive about promoting yourself or your commercial potential to the public. There is a right and a wrong way to successfully promote yourself. I know a lot of real estate agents who think it's appropriate to simply promote their smiling faces, but that kind of promotion actually turns a lot of people off. You have to create a "buzz," but you have to do it productively so the public will key in on your message, and most important, you have to actually have a message. It can't be hollow buzz; it must contain real substance.

You're good at what you do; you've spent a lot of time developing your skills and learning the intricacies of your trade. You've experienced a sequence of events that no one else in the world has ever experienced the same way you have, and you've taken a particular path to get to the professional level you are today. You have to learn to embrace the path you've taken, learn from your experiences, figure out what makes you different and promote these factors. It sounds elementary, but most people don't realize that they aren't letting their potential customers and surrounding marketplace know what they're good at and why they are the right choice.

Every day we see companies in the news that are releasing new products or starting new initiatives. Most people don't realize it, but these companies are actually feeding the media outlets, whether local or national, the news they want people to know about. News editors normally don't go out searching for this information; it is delivered to them through press releases. So you, as the business owner or manager, can control your own positioning by creating news releases, and it works the same, whether you run a large or small business. You can release your news online through a variety of websites; I personally like www.prweb.com or www.prlog.com. You should also post your news on your own website. Controlling your own news releases allows you to position yourself in any manner and in any direction you desire.

The 5th Power Principle: Control Your Communication—Don't Let It Control You

The biggest lie of the 21st century is that technology will make your life easier. Our cell phones, BlackBerrys and laptop computers that we use everywhere through Wi-Fi connections are taking up more of our time than they probably should. Technology is never going to make your life easier; instead technology will definitely make your life busier. When I say busier, I don't mean more productive. Most of your day is spent simply doing busy work. We even set daily deadlines and, in many times, by the end of the day you probably didn't complete the task. We perceive that we are so busy that most tasks in our lives take a back seat and nothing ever gets done. We've all heard someone say during the day, "I'm just so busy all day! I get all these emails and phone calls and that kept me so busy I just couldn't get anything done." Before long we've waited a day, a week, a month or a year without getting anything long accomplished. We often don't set aside time to complete the projects we need to finish, and these tasks are usually much more important than most of the emails we get caught up in responding to.

When someone owns a business, of course, they want to make their clients happy. But in order to keep a consistent level of customer support that will follow us no matter how busy we get, we need to set boundaries of when we answer the phone and when we respond to emails. Your clients pay you a fee to do a job for them, and chances are you have more than one client. You need to communicate effectively with each one, but don't get caught up in bad habits like responding instantly to every single email. This becomes unmanageable when you have more than a handful of clients. If you constantly respond to inquiries, you will find that you have less time to actually do what you've been hired to do. You need to be able to devote your full time and attention to each client's project and not be constantly distracted. Tell clients how you work up front, so their expectations will be met, kindly ask them to leave a message, and assure them that you will be professional about calling them back. Let your customers know that if it's an emergency, they are welcome to call your cell phone. But set your personal boundaries because if you don't remove yourself from the hustle and bustle of simply being busy, you'll never accomplish anything. You have to take a break from the BlackBerry or the cell phone now and then. Otherwise, you will feel like you're working 24 hours a day.

It sounds silly, and we all deny that we fall into this category, but we can't forget the fact that we also have personal lives that must be balanced with our day-to-day professional responsibilities.

Someone recently asked me how I balance everything I have going on in my life. I will tell you it is a constant struggle for me, but using these tactics helps me immensely. If I just "stay busy," it looks like I'm doing a ton of work, but I might be completing a quarter of the work I'm capable of accomplishing. We have to understand that while email is a revolutionary tool, it can also be dangerous to our productivity. It is a great tool for certain situations, but for most of us it has become more of a distraction than a productive way of communicating. We have all written a 30-minute email response that should have been condensed to say, "Thanks for the invitation but I can't make it this time," but instead we get wrapped up in trying to communicate through email and trying to get our tone across, but that is no easy task. Everyone reads things based on the mood they are in when it comes across their desk. If we would have just picked up the phone, we would have had much less risk of hurting the other person's feelings, and it would have taken us one-tenth of the time it took to draft a long, drawn-out email. It seems to be a foreign concept these days, but sometimes you should just pick up the phone. If you analyze your communications to make sure you are being as effective as possible, you find that, in the right situations, if you pick up the phone rather than fire off an email, you will find more time to do other things. And that's just one small example. The key here is to analyze your communication and make proactive decisions to control it, rather than letting it control you.

The 6th Power Principle: Get Accountable

In order to become an effective and objective businessperson in today's 21st century commercial climate, you must take responsibility for the things that occur in your life, good or bad. The best way to get accountable to yourself and your business is to become accountable to others. I really advocate joining or creating a group of like-minded individuals who are in a similar industry or who are looking to forge ahead and receive more rewards in their business life. Set up monthly group meetings with people who are targeting the same goals in their lives as you are. Brainstorm and discuss the projects you are working on. You'll soon find out that when you outwardly share your goals with your peers one month, if you show up at the next meeting without accomplishing your objectives, you'll not only feel like you let yourself down, but you'll also feel like you let the members of your accountability group down. This type of environment creates a healthy kind of peer pressure and a sense of camaraderie that forces you to get things done.

Find people who you enjoy being with, and that you don't mind sharing information with, and make yourself accountable to them. It's a great way to motivate yourself because you'll be anxious to get to the next meeting to let everyone know what you've accomplished. This is a really great way to accelerate your success.

The 7th Power Principle: Sell Information

In today's business world, everyone has the opportunity to become an expert because everyone has a certain amount of specialized information in their head. When we talk about other concepts of scalability and positioning, it ties into the fact that if you can take your information and turn it into something tangible, like a written newsletter or a compact disc, you can sell it or use it as a tool to gain new customers. Let's take another example, a personal trainer. This is a great way to prospect and a great way to make some extra money. If the personal trainer is really getting better results for their clients in half the time, they've probably created a system for accomplishing this. While the system may not be anything completely new, or it may be a combination of other systems, if this trainer can find a way to put their "spin" on it, they will reach a group of people who most likely no one has reached before. We all connect with different types of people, and there is room for more personalities in the marketplace because you just don't know who is ready to learn from someone like you, and all there is only one "you." Instead of just keeping this system in the trainer's head and making money implementing it for clients, why not write down the system, include all the collateral materials they're using, including marketing materials, client intake forms, client progress reports, workout summaries, and anything else they've created, and then sell that system to other personal trainers. At that point, not only is the personal trainer a business-to-consumer solution, but now the trainer has figured out a way to become a valuable source of information for other businesses as well. He has added a business-to-business component. Not to mention that you could sell a version of this product to consumers as well who would rather work out on their own, without the cost of a trainer. Using this strategy, you can instantly create another income stream.

You can make money by selling your informational system or by giving pieces of it away to prospective clients to show them your level of knowledge and competency. At that point, you become the expert in your field. People always ask me, "How does someone become an expert?" And the true response is, you tell people you're an expert. Even more powerful is if you can get other people to tell everyone you're an expert, and you can do this through the use of third-party testimonials. Another great vehicle to becoming an expert is to write a book on a chosen topic. If you write a book and someone has taken the time to read it, then you've got a great opportunity to gain a customer; it is as if you just spent hour after hour speaking directly to them. By this time, they've certainly connected with you and decided whether they like you or not and to them you are the expert from that moment on.

The 8th Power Principle: Breakthroughs

Now that you've started from scratch, developed your tools, understood the concepts of effective communications, written your book and joined the necessary support groups in the local area, the next step is to reap the harvest of what you've created. We all want as many "breakthroughs" as possible for our businesses because that's where we make money. You've learned your whole life that you must first go to first grade, then to second grade, and that you just need to take things one step at a time. Well, while you still have to go through grade school that way for the most part, I'm here to tell you that in the real world, that's a lie! Don't believe it. What you should do is take massive action. Let's say you want to start implementing some of these steps; don't take them one at a time—do them all! You won't be great at all of them at first, but if you start working on all eight of these Power Principles simultaneously, it will come together much faster. If you start working on one principle a month for eight months, think about how long it will take you before you can start making things happen. That's how you create breakthroughs while your profit potential begins to grow exponentially. Keep in mind, you must stay focused.

Begin developing a lifestyle vs. a "workstyle." Massive action is what makes this system work. If you plan to send out a postcard soliciting business from new clients, try many different versions to see which one works best. Massive action produces breakthroughs. If you only send out one copy or one version, you'll never know whether it was a great or not.

If you own a business, of course, you want it to be profitable. The difference between a great company and a good company can be measured through solid innovative thinking, a positive attitude, and the passion to make a difference in your niche. You have to actively participate to make things happen. Realistically not all of these principles will work in every business, and some things won't always work the first time you try them. Have backup plans, create a cash reserve, and try to set up something you know is consistent. However, if you're up for the challenge, take massive action using the Power Principles for 30 days in a row. I bet you will see an increase in your income, and at the very worst, you will learn a few lessons along the way about what works and what doesn't. Remember, there is risk in everything, but without risk, there is no reward.

Most important, have faith in yourself. You got into business because you trusted your gut, and you know you are good at what you do. Never second-guess yourself on that point and keep pressing on because quite often the most successful businessperson is simply the most persistent.

Acknowledgements

There are many people who contribute to what an author finally puts down on paper, and I have been fortunate to know people who are always willing to share ideas that they believe set one business apart from another.

What appears in this book as my ideas have really come from friends, mentors and business associates who shared and conveyed the vision that it is a "person" who can truly give life to a product or service. "People buy people" who they know, like and trust, and if you build a personality-driven business, the customer will make a stronger and faster connection with you.

David Edmunds, my father-in-law, was one of the first who taught me this business concept, teaching me a simple lesson about putting your picture and personal information on a special folded business card he designed for his real estate salesmen. He thought the personal touch was so important he actually bought his own printing press and made personalized stationary for each of his salesmen with their photos on it. This was a very important idea to him because it was 42 years ago, and you couldn't just run down to your local Kinko's and get it done. It took time and extra money, but he knew it made a difference because it helped people "remember you, and you stand apart when they see your picture," he always said.

David's idea was not my last lesson about the importance of developing yourself as a personality for your product or service, and each time I forgot to do so it cost me money. Over the years, I have spent tens of millions of dollars proving this idea, and I hope this book can save you from learning the lesson the expensive way and allow you to make money faster.

My thanks to Linda, my wife of 41 years, for being the special person she is to me and our family. She is the glue that holds us all together and keeps our family strong. The greatest sale I ever made was convincing her to be with me on this wonderful journey we are on together.

To Nick, Lindsay and Greg, thanks for being great partners in this very exciting and rewarding business we have and continue to grow. Your energy, passion, and skill sets are unique and limitless, and I look forward to expanding the vision we all share for helping others achieve their best.

—JW

Wow, now that we're in the second printing of this book, I can truly say that I never imagined the journey it would take me on! And for that I'm extremely humbled and thankful. I would be remiss if I didn't take this opportunity to say "Thank You" to God for guiding me in all things that I do and for sending your Son to give us all a chance to live eternally— and with as much fun as it is here on earth, I can only imagine what you've got in store for us up there.

Kristina, my wife, partner and best friend, for listening to my crazy ideas all the time and not sending me to the loony bin. I love you and could not do any of the things I do without your support. Thanks for not giving up on me and making me realize that the best things in life are often standing right in front of you begging you to notice them. You are a beautiful person inside and out, and I'm always proud to have you on my arm. Also, I can never thank you enough for our three little ones. The party is just beginning!

Brock, Bowen and Addison, although you are still in the earliest portion of your lives, I'm more proud of you than anything I've ever created in my life, and I can't wait for you all to show the world what you've got to offer. I love you all dearly and can't wait to spend lots of time showing you how to live, laugh and love, and hope I can be half the parent that my parents were to me.

Mum and Dad, wow, where to begin. You have both always been my biggest fans and have gone through more with me than I can ever thank you for. The two of you are undoubtedly the two finest human beings that I will ever get a chance to know, and I'm amazingly proud to call you my parents. The mark you are leaving on people in this world with your unwavering love and dedication as well as your willingness to always "lend a hand, as well as an ear" will transcend all that you could possibly imagine. The two of you single-handedly make the world a better place one day at a time. I love you both dearly and can't thank you enough.

Andy, it's been amazing growing up with you. You've been my role model since I was old enough to know that you were my big brother, and you've always found ways to make me work harder, really think things through and challenge the status quo. Thanks for always being there and teaching me some of the most important lessons in life.

Jack, I can never thank you enough for your willingness to take me under your wing and teach me about business, but more important, about life. I owe this accomplishment and many others to you. I hope one day to be able to teach someone else a fraction of the lessons you have taught me. Your kindness, generosity and willingness to help never go unnoticed. Thanks for helping me feel like I'm not the only crazy person in this world—now I know there are at least two of us! I look forward to much more success for which I will continue to say, "Thank you."

Lindsay and Greg, you guys have magnified everything we do, and I'm so glad to have you guys on board. Thanks for helping us grow this vision to "Help the Most People, Help the Most People."

—Nick

As a child what I wanted to do when I "grew up" wasn't the question; it was how I would get there that seemed to be fuzzy and filled with dead-ends. Although school turned out to be vastly important in my journey for many reasons, including meeting my husband, it never seemed like it at the time. But if it wasn't for school and the love of the people around me, I wouldn't be where I am today.

Mrs. Goggin and Mrs. Pitman, you taught me more than math, the English language and the literary works of the great, you taught me to believe in myself and that my learning disabilities would not, and could not, limit me as a person. You gave me strength and confidence in myself despite my challenges and saw something in me that no other teacher had ever taken the time to notice—a student with the will to do great, but just had a little trouble getting there. Thank you both for taking the chance on me and for your encouragement. Mrs. Pitman, I still use the word "plethora" in just about every piece that I write. Who knew I'd be an author... and a multi-best-selling author at that! I bet you did. Thank you.

Momma and Daddy, you have loved me from the day I was born and every day in between. Daddy, you are my father, my mentor, my business partner and so much more. Thank you for your love, support and guidance through this crazy journey. Momma, thank you for always going the extra mile to let me know how much I was loved. Without you, I wouldn't be the woman I am today, both in business and as a wife.

Eric, you are my husband, my partner, my best friend, my support, the love of my life and everything I am not. Thank you for your constant love and unwavering support. I could not do what I do without you standing next to me. I love you.

"I can do all things through Him who gives me strength."
Philippians 4:13

—Lindsay

I would like to thank my wife Jennifer for pushing me from the moment I met her to share my ideas with the world. I'll never forget the late nights working, writing, studying, traveling and struggling to create a better future for our family. I can never repay you for the strength you have given me, and ultimately, making me into the man that I am today.

To Colten, I loved you from the minute I saw you. It's not often that one second in our lives can change everything about your entire world, but you my son, did. I am anxious to show you the world, spoil you rotten, and teach you everything I know about taking care of people, listening, learning, and growing into a young man that the world cannot stop.

Mom, even though you aren't here today, I know you give me the ideas and drive to keep going. If only you could see how far we've come. You would have a never-ending smile from ear to ear.

Dad, your continued support means the world to me. Teaching me how to compete, how to rise to the occasion and how to be open to all ideas, opinions and situations allows me to think clear, to think through problems and make the best of any situation.

Brian, you are more inspirational than you may think. My little brother, you teach me more about life every time we talk. Everything we did as kids made us into the people that we are now, and I wouldn't have it any other way!

Rich and Janet, you two have come into my life and been inspiring, loving and caring since the day I took your daughter out when we were 16. You are both actually the reason I have gotten into this crazy entrepreneurial dream I find myself in today and for that I am forever grateful (on top of giving me the love of my life).

Jack and Nick, I have to thank you for welcoming me into your families as well. The purpose, direction and motivation you have given me has allowed us all to impact more lives, businesses and families, and together we can keep building on the dream to help the most people—a mission that I hold deep in my heart. Thank you.

—*Greg*

More Celebrity Branding® for You!

Just as those of you who are successful in life and in business know that you can't expect to stay at the top of your industry if you relax once you reach the pinnacle of success, we also know that you will need to stay on top of your Celebrity Branding® process. In order to make this easy for you, we've created www.DNAgency.com so you can keep up with all the newest tips and strategies that we uncover as we continue to work with some of the biggest and best Experts in business.

Be sure to visit www.DNAgency.com to sign up for our free CelebrityZine™ as well as to find many great resources that you can use so you won't be left behind. We look forward to hearing about your success and welcome your correspondence.

We can be reached at:
Info@DNAgency.com
(800) 980-1626

The
Dicks + Nanton Celebrity Branding Agency® Resources

The Dicks + Nanton Celebrity Branding Agency® Resources

Become the Recognized Celebrity Expert® in Your Field!

A Celebrity Expert® is a master in the art of living

"A master in the art of living draws no sharp distinction between his work and his play, his mind and his body, his education and his recreation. He hardly knows which is which. He simply pursues his vision or excellence through whatever he is doing and leaves others to determine whether he is working or playing. To himself, he always seems to be doing both." —James A. Michener

This year has seen the Dicks + Nanton Celebrity Branding Agency®, as well as our clients live that very statement, from beginning the year with 40 amazing clients and their spouses and friends at the 2012 Grammy Awards to placing bets with Dan Kennedy at the Kentucky Derby to shooting documentaries at LSU baseball games and in State Governors' homes. We have introduced new legends to our group of Celebrity Experts® like Jack Canfield and Tom Hopkins and will release two new books with our friend and mentor, Brian Tracy.

Inside the pages of your *Celebrity Expert® Insider Special Edition* is a look into not just our world and the things we do to help over a thousand Celebrity Experts® in 26 countries but at how Dicks + Nanton Celebrity Branding Agency® can change both your business and your life. Steak dinners transition into Red Carpet premiers. Tri-fold brochures become shock-and-awe packages that win you business time and time again from your strongest competition who just don't get it. Websites become living, breathing parts of your business that attract the part of your market that is ready to take action with you today. And, yes, your life will forever be changed once you add the irreplaceable title of Best-Selling Author to your arsenal.

So take a look, dream, imagine and live out the words that James A. Michener wrote above. Once you do, your life will never be the same.

Nick, Jack, Lindsay and Greg

The Dicks + Nanton Celebrity Branding Agency®

Be Seen on ABC, NBC, CBS and FOX Affiliates Across the Country

One thing that separates our Agency from other Media, Marketing or PR films is that we **guarantee** our results.

And we also guarantee that you will have a great time in the process. Every year we host 6 to 9 of our own branded TV Shows across the country to highlight and tell your story. From the "Brian Tracy Show" to "The New Masters of Real Estate," "Health and Wellness Today" and "America's PremierExperts®," we have shows that suit every entrepreneur, professional small business owner, author or expert. Appearances on these shows position you as both an expert and a thought leader in your field.

Our TV shoots are unlike any event you have ever attended. From the atmosphere to the media training, from the professional photo shoot to the three-camera live interview, this experience is one you will remember for the rest of your life. Every detail is taken care of for you, from preparation to editing, from makeup to giving you the media credentials that would take a lifetime to get on your own. In addition, you will receive press releases, a hi-def copy of your interview, and more than 50 ways to use the video, the logos and the credibility in your business to get your story, your passion and your emotion into the hands of more people than ever before.

Our next TV season is casting now, and the only way to guarantee yourself media placement on the biggest networks on the planet is to call your Business Agent® at **888-592-0062** today. We look forward to seeing you on set!

Become a Best-Selling Author

Once you become a client of the Dicks + Nanton Celebrity Branding Agency®, our singular goal in business is to help you become a Celebrity Expert® in your marketplace. The most effective way to do that is to become a published author, and even better yet, a Best-Selling Author. As an agency client, we will get you signed to a publishing contract with

CelebrityPress® Publishing to work on your own book or join one of our multi-author books with other Celebrity Experts®.

Over the past five years we have helped over 800 clients from all over the world not only become published authors but also elevated their status to Best-Selling Author. We guarantee we can do it for you too!

Over the past year we have given our clients the opportunity to co-author books with legends such as Brian Tracy, Tom Hopkins, Jack Canfield, Dan Kennedy, Michael E. Gerber, Dr. Ivan Misner, Mari Smith and others. Writing, releasing and including these books in your marketing is the most powerful way to develop yourself into a Celebrity Expert® and position yourself as the go-to person in your field.

If you are looking to become a published author of your own book or with other co-authors, speak with one of our Business Agents® today to talk about how we can guarantee your book is a Best-Seller and you become a Best-Selling Author! Call **888-592-0062** today and speak with your Business Agent®.

The National Academy of Best-Selling Authors®

Writing a book is one of the greatest ways to give back. Taking that book and marketing it to the world so that it becomes a Best-Seller creates an impact and positions you as a thought leader in your field. In 2010, Nick and JW launched the National Academy of Best-Selling Authors® to recognize and honor the works of authors who have achieved Best-Seller status.

The Academy has inducted over 800 authors, including legends such as Brian Tracy, Michael E. Gerber, Jack Canfield and entrepreneurs and experts just like you who have reached the monumental status of Best-Selling Author!

As part of the National Academy of Best-Selling Authors®, we hold an annual event, The Best-Seller's Summit and Golden Gala Awards to recognize the accomplishments of Best-Selling Authors. In 2012, we were honored to present the 3rd annual Best-Seller's Summit and Golden Gala Awards right in the heart of Hollywood at the historic Roosevelt Hotel, the site of the first Academy Awards.

Every year we gather Best-Selling Authors from across the world to award them our Quilly Statue, which is made by the same group that produces the Oscars and the Grammy Awards! The event is an opportunity to learn from the world's top thought leaders and join in a celebration of entrepreneurship and authorship with a group of peers who have elevated their status to Best-Selling Author.

If you are a Best-Selling Author or become one with our help, you will be invited to a once-in-a-lifetime Red Carpet experience to recognize your accomplishments. Reserve your seat now or get pre-registered for our 2013 event by speaking with your Business Agent® today.

BigPrint® Media Exposure

What you do in your business and how you help your clients is a story worth telling the world about. In our BigPrint® Media Campaigns, we help you do just that and place your story in major media publications as well as hundreds of dot-coms across the web.

I'm sure you have heard the expression "content is King" when it comes to marketing your business online. In our BigPrint® Packages, we help you create content that is extremely valuable, developing links back to your website and bringing you media credibility in the process.

Our team of expert writers begin by interviewing you and crafting a core story about you and your business. This is a big-time feature article and is a story that you can use well after this campaign ends. The story is then syndicated online, and we get a quote, link and image from you to place in one of the print media we are working with, from *USA Today*, to the *Wall Street Journal* or even *Inc.* magazine. Many of our clients frame the "tear sheets" that run in these publications and have them hanging in their offices in recognition of their appearance.

Additionally, every month our team will follow up with you to write press releases about you and your business to syndicate online, again creating more and more content for you. This package is truly the symbol of using media, marketing and PR together to grow your business.

Contact your Business Agent® today at **888-592-0062** to see how you can join us in an opportunity to showcase you in our next BigPrint® Campaign!

The Celebrity Expert® Mastermind Experience

Napoleon Hill famously wrote in his classic book *Think and Grow Rich*:

"Economic advantages may be created by any person who surrounds himself with the advice, counsel, and personal cooperation of a group of men who are willing to lend him wholehearted aid, in a spirit of PERFECT HARMONY. This form of cooperative alliance has been the basis of nearly every great fortune. Your understanding of this great truth may definitely determine your financial status."

We have found this statement to be true in our own business. It is why we continually surround ourselves with coaches, experts and mentors like Brian Tracy or Dan Kennedy. It's why we continually go to events all over the world to learn, meet new people and engage in new experiences.

The Celebrity Expert® Mastermind experiences, however, are unlike anything you have ever been a part of!

- Have you ever ridden a scooter around the island of Bermuda while talking about your marketing materials?

- What about getting your expansion ideas heard and assessed by lawyers, doctors, consultants and our Executive Team?

- Have you closed a deal while listening to Paul McCartney or Bruce Springsteen at the Grammy Awards?

- We have even created lifelong partnerships and friendships while betting on funny horse names at the Kentucky Derby.

In the past two years, we have taken an exclusive group of Celebrity Experts® with us to work, engage, open up, come clean, and leave with clarity and inspiration to how they are going to live out the life of a Celebrity Expert®. We come together in formal meetings, take notes and consume ideas until our hands are tired and our brains cannot take anymore.

Our Mastermind programs are small-group experiences unlike any other and are limited. If you would like to apply to join this exclusive group that travels and learns in some of the most fun locations in the world, please email **Info@DNAgency.com** today or call your Business Agent® at **888-592-0062**

Let Us Build Your Digital DNA

What happens when a customer or prospect Googles your name or the name of your business? Do you like the results? Would you like to own those results like a true Celebrity Expert®? Online Marketing Expert Lindsay Dicks has developed online branding, content and website strategies for hundreds of Celebrity Experts® across the world, and you could be next.

Today, your "credibility" is based on what appears in search engine results. And, unfortunately, not having any results (or just your website) can be just as damaging as bad results because you are invisible to your prospects.

We understand that in today's online world, your web presence is much more than just a website (although, you better have one of those, too!). Your online brand is EVERY piece of content out there on the internet. Our proven system not only showcases your expert status and dominates the search engine results, but it will help you suppress any negative listings you may have that are hurting you.

Our Digital DNA Packages range from website design to total turnkey online marketing systems and are priced according to your needs.

• Custom website design

• Content writing services with search engine optimization

• Blog writing and syndication

• Press release writing and syndication

• Social media marketing

• Micro-sites

- Link building

- And more

To see how you stack up with your Digital DNA and to finally create a website that attracts business and brings new prospects into your sales funnel, request a website and online marketing review today by calling us at **800-989-5690** or contacting Lindsay at **Info@CelebritySites.com**.

A Full Documentary Film Production... Starring YOU!

Nothing captivates someone quite like a movie. It's why we have been spending Friday and Saturday nights eating popcorn, drinking soda pop, and watching movies on the big screen since 1896!

Coming from his entertainment background, Nick always dreamed of producing a feature film. And it just so happened that a great group of clients were not only able to finance his first film with him, but they helped him earn an Emmy for Best Director along the way.

That first film was "Jacob's Turn," a story about a 4-year-old boy with Down Syndrome playing in his first baseball game. The documentary was released in 2010 and earned Nick an Emmy for Director. Since then, Nick and the entire Agency have caught movie fever. In 2011, Celebrity Films released "Car Men," a documentary about used-car dealer Tracy Myers. The film has been a game changer for both Nick and Tracy, and a new way of telling stories about businesses through film was born.

In fact, the documentaries have become a movement, with over 10 clients signed for the upcoming months, including a new series on the Biography Channel called "Profiles of Success®."

The Celebrity Films experience is a full 2-day shoot full of excitement and anticipation for you, your staff and everyone in your community. Words cannot do justice to the impact that these films can have on your business, from throwing local movie screenings for all your clients at a rented-out theater to being featured on "Profiles of Success" on the Biography Channel.

To see the latest film trailer and to schedule an appointment to talk about creating a film about your business, please visit **www.CelebrityFilms.com**.

Market Yourself Like a Celebrity Expert®

Over the past five years, we have not only helped over 1,500 clients become Celebrity Experts® through media, marketing and PR, but we have also developed the best products and processes to market Celebrity Experts® to their target market.

For the first time ever, we are opening up our marketing team to you. Not only are we bringing you the best media, marketing and PR opportunities outlined in this catalog, but we are going to help you use each and every piece and create a turnkey marketing campaign to attract your home-run clients, close more business, and truly become the definitive Celebrity Expert® in your marketplace. This unique marketing process is broken down into 6 steps which comprise the Celebrity Expert® Marketing System.

STEP ❶ **Your Business And Marketing Assessment**

STEP ❷ **Core Story Media Creation**

STEP ❸ Lead Capturing And Database Management

STEP ❹ Automated Lead Nurturing

STEP ❺ New Client Acquisition

STEP ❻ Client Retention And Referral Based Marketing

You Are No Longer Guessing, Hoping or Stringing Pieces Together

The best part of the Celebrity Expert® Marketing System is that we do everything for you. From content creation to copywriting, list management and sequencing, we will build a marketing process and system just like ours but custom tailored for you and your market.

Best yet, for a limited time, you can lock in your own exclusive territory for us to work with just you in your business niche and market. Imagine taking our proven Celebrity Expert® Marketing System, having it run your marketing, and at the same time keeping out your competition.

Get started by giving our CMO, Greg Rollett, a call at **888-592-0062** or email him at **Greg@DNAgency.com**.

Dianne Black

"I have found the *Celebrity Branding You®* book very helpful, very easy to read, clear to the point, without any fluff and unnecessary jargon to pad it out. The authors obviously know their subject. Anyone looking to groom themselves, to make the best of themselves, in whatever business they enter into would do very well to use this book as a resource."

Iminay

"*Celebrity Branding You®* offers actionable, practical advice on how to find your niche, your expertise—and then lists the step-by-step strategies for how to maximize marketing media exposure and "hits" so you quickly scale to Celebrity Status and arrive at the top of the Google search results.

With real-life examples and web references throughout, this book offers value from start to finish. For a book supposedly written by two lawyers, there is no legalese… easy to read and understand. Couldn't put it down. Read in one night to get the gist of the book, now I'll go over it again more slowly and start highlighting websites to check out. Recommend to all who want to generate leads and drive results. Delivers on its title."

Brett Burky

"The team at Dicks + Nanton Agency have created a book that will remain in my books that I read yearly. The ideas they give for someone wanting to further themselves in their career are excellent. It is a whole package book, a blueprint for taking yourself from a nobody in your industry to the industry name. Highly recommended."

Sean Barker (Labrador City, NL)

"This book is a very easy read and is the ultimate blueprint for creating a business that is successful and authentic based on you. Most people don't realize the value of expressing their individuality when creating their business. *Celebrity Branding You®* shows you all the steps you need to take to build a business brand based on the most valuable person in your business, YOU. After reading most business books out there I would highly recommend this book for its content and valuable resources."

Eric G. Lancaster (Tucson, AZ)

"*Celebrity Branding You®* has tons of tips and links that help guide any entrepreneur toward effective branding strategies. What is great about the book is that it is so easy and straight forward. I would recommend it for anyone who is involved in a business and wants some good pointers they may have missed in other books."

Blake Harris (Gainesville, FL)

"*Celebrity Branding You®* is a must for any small business owner looking to grow their business. In their book, *Celebrity Branding You®*, Jack Dicks and Nick Nanton teach how anyone can become the best in their industry.

Celebrity Branding You® takes the concepts from *Rich Dad Poor Dad* and gives clear and simple instructions to implement for any entrepreneur. If you are looking to grow your company or learn how to become an entrepreneur and you read only one book this year, this should be it."

Paul Seago

"This is truly one of the best books on branding yourself and your business on the market today.

"In fact, the first words of the book are one of the most important rules of business and one that is often most overlooked: people buy people. That is so true. People may not know how good your product is if they don't get to know you and build a relationship.

Jack and Nick also lay out exactly how to develop your celebrity image and how to gain credibility. No one else is giving this kind of helpful, detailed information. I have started using some of the tools described in the book, and I can tell you it works.

Do yourself and your business a favor—buy this book, read it, and do the things they say!"

Michael McDevitt (Thousand Oaks, CA)

"There is no doubt about it, if you implement the advice of JW and Nick in their book *Celebrity Branding You®*, you will definitely stand out from your competition. Very captivating—a good read!"

Gordie Allen (Killarney, FL)

"Celebrity Branding You® provides wanna-be celebrities a comprehensive, tactical blueprint for establishing their unique brand in a very competitive marketplace. Each chapter is replete with techniques and specific resources for moving the process to a successful conclusion. As a professional sales trainer, speaker and consultant for 26 years, I recommend this book to anyone who aims to fast-track their celebrity branding goals."

Marianne Laudati (West Palm Beach, FL)

"The best and most comprehensive marketing book I have ever read. Applicable to any profession or industry. Detailed info on online marketing especially enlightening. I highly recommend this book for anyone who wants to outshine the competition and rise to the top in their field. A necessary read for those who want to not only survive but prosper in these tough economic times."

Zalon (Solo Recording Artist and Touring Member of Amy Winehouse's Band)

"Your book, Celebrity Branding You®, is absolutely AMAZING. I read 75 percent on the first night and stayed up till 9 am in the morning reading before forcing myself to sleep."

J. J. Ketterling

"Celebrity Branding You® lays down the exact blue print to get you above and beyond any competition. Times have changed and so has marketing, and these guys nailed it!"

Gregg Stebben

"…if you already understand that you don't have to be Bono or Oprah to benefit from being a celebrity in your own world or industry or community.

And if you DO want to be a celebrity on the scale of Bono or Oprah…this book will help too.

It tells you what to do and how to do it…and now it's time for you to get out there and do it!"

William "Pat" Rigsby

"JW Dicks and Nick Nanton have created the definitive guide to becoming the 'go to' expert in your field in *Celebrity Branding You*®. They've not only explained the logic behind branding yourself, but they provide you with a comprehensive blueprint that will allow you to become a celebrity.

If you own a business, aspire to own a business or just want to be positioned as an expert, *Celebrity Branding You*® is a must read."

Dan Liebrecht and Tony Dietsch
Clean Guru LLC

"Jack and Nick,

Wow! I just finished reading your new book, *Celebrity Branding You*®, and it's simply great!

Your personalities, energy and ethics 'jump off the page.'

The reader quickly learns celebrity branding isn't an exercise in out-of-control egotism but rather a practical and proven strategy for growth.

Tony and I are lucky to have found two legal and marketing

mentors as terrific as you guys!

We're determined to become your biggest Celebrity Branding Success Story ever… and help thousands of others along the way!

Thanks, from two raving fans!"

Arel Moodie (New York)

"What's cool about this book is that it helped to understand that you can "Brand" yourself however you want. You are in control of the image you send out there, by way of creating your online presence and how to create credibility indicators. I'm still going through it but, so far I'm very pleased!"

Bernice Allen (Orlando, FL)

"**What a great read!** I have only read the first few chapters and can already tell you that this is a GREAT read! I was fortunate enough to meet Nick at a networking event last week. Anyone who runs their own business should have a copy and should read it. I mean, really read it. Looking forward to becoming my very own celebrity brand!"

Beverly Ewan (Bronx, New York)

"*Celebrity Branding You*® by Nick Nanton and JW Dicks explodes with information. The authors are lawyers by trade with over 50 years combined working experience.

I read this book in one day and was surprised how easy it was to read, and more important, it made sense. I understand why they started by saying, "People buy People"; the concept applies to any business with products or services.

I liked how the chapters are laid out; it shows that the authors were thinking of the reader and made it easy to understand by starting at the beginning of the marketing process. Each chapter then takes you through the process step by step, with reliable resources they have used and examples and case studies.

I recommend this book to anyone who is struggling with their marketing plan (or lacks a plan). If you learn what Dicks & Nanton are teaching in this book, soon you will become a branded expert and clients or customers will find you because you stand out."

Randy Friedman

"*Celebrity Branding You*® is a fabulous book. Not only is it an interesting read (I couldn't put it down), but it makes so much sense. For myself, I know the only way to build my business as a Corporate Golf Professional and author of *Your Inner Swing* is to get my name out there and 'brand' myself in the corporate world. Because I've never had a plan for becoming the guru in my business laid out so clearly in front of me, I've been floundering. You give precise methods and ways for someone like myself to get up and running like a pro. It's brilliant!! Thanks!"

Felicia Caldwell Gopaul

"Many entrepreneurs instinctively understand the value of becoming a celebrity to their target market but have no idea how they can systematically achieve that goal.

Celebrity Branding You® provides a game plan that business owners can follow to build their expert celebrity status.

If becoming a client attraction magnet is your goal as a business owner, then do more than read the book with highlighter in hand. IMPLEMENT and see what becoming a celebrity to your niche market can do for your business!"

John Hinds (Newark, NJ)

"JW Dicks and Nick Nanton have touched on a topic that is often overlooked by most entrepreneurs. *Celebrity Branding You®* provides you with a well-thought-out game plan on how you can become the celebrity expert in your niche.

First, the book provided an important reminder about the fact that "People Buy People." Sometimes, we as business owners get wrapped up in the product or service that we're marketing and lose sight of this fact.

Another section of the book that I found valuable was the idea of putting your story behind your brand. In other words, "Why Do You Do What You Do?" If the only answers that come up are "I am doing it for the money" or "Because this is what I've always done," then you may need to rethink your whole motivation behind your particular business or find a business that has real meaning to you.

The authors then cover the ever-important topic regarding your website. They provided some excellent advice on branding your site and solidifying your celebrity status in your niche.

Finally, the authors provided the 'Top 10 Ways to Grow Your Business Fast.' They provided some excellent strategies in this section.

All in all, I highly recommend that you not only get a copy of this book, but more important, take action on the ideas presented in it.

So what are you waiting for?

BE SOMEBODY!"

Mark J. Beck (Long Valley, NJ)

"*Celebrity Branding You®* is a no-nonsense, to-the-point

resource for finding and creating your own celebrity brand. It's full of both online and offline strategies to make this process as easy as possible.

I just had the pleasure of hearing Nick Nanton speak to a group of entrepreneurs in New Jersey, and I can tell you that he really gets it. All budding entrepreneurs should read this book and get a jump start on their competition."

Mark Ijlal

Michigan Foreclosure Report

"The Shortcut to Becoming a Rock Star in Your Niche!

We live in a celebrity-crazy culture. Heck even the top 10 searches in Google are all about Paris and Britney. So it is fitting that JW Dicks and Nick Nanton have written an incredibly practical blueprint on how to make yourself famous and a celebrity brand in your industry and niche.

It is all here—from finding your niche, building a profitable website with a complete marketing plan, creating your personal brand and expert status, finding and promoting your story in both online and offline worlds.

I am implementing these strategies in my own consulting business right now in Michigan, and I am already seeing major changes in the way my new clients are attracted to my personal brand.

Your clients want a celebrity. You need to become one. Buy this book. You will know how to do it step by step."

Bill Glazer, President

Glazer-Kennedy Insider's Circle™

"JW Dicks and Nick Nanton, in their book, reveal one of the true business secrets that practically all entrepreneurs miss…which is to brand yourself. At Glazer-Kennedy Insider's Circle (dankennedy.com), we have been teaching for years that you want to run a celebrity-driven business and what's more important is to make yourself the celebrity! In *Celebrity Branding You*®, they do a superb job of walking you through this invaluable process, from A-Z. This is a must read for every business owner and entrepreneur."

Alex K. Tchekmeian, CEO, AKT Enterprises
Listed in *Businessweek*'s "America's Best Young Entrepreneurs 2007"

"Jack and Nick are the best in the business at turning entrepreneurs and businesspeople into celebrities, and this book lays out a step-by-step plan in a clear and informative way. Throughout the past few years, Jack and Nick have helped me identify a lot of the things in business that I may have overlooked [by] being such a young entrepreneur. Their words and advice have now been expressed in writing for the entire world to hear. I highly recommend this book to anybody interested in becoming known as a taste-making business owner, artist or entrepreneur."

Dicks + Nanton Agency Testimonials

Jim Stacey (Adrian, MI)

"In all my business dealings with Nick Nanton, I have found him to be a man of high integrity. When issues come up for clarification, he steps up to the plate and delivers customer service rarely seen in today's business world. I wrote the chapter on customer service in the book, *Win*. Nick has met and exceeded those principles."

Alex Wathen, Esq (Houston, TX)

"Emmy award-winning public relations expert Nick Nanton and his Dicks + Nanton Agency team has done an outstanding job propelling me into the spotlight. Using his proven strategies and track record for success, he has, in a short time, not only made me a best-selling author through an excellent book deal, [but] he has also made me the Bankruptcy Expert Blogger at *FastCompany*. I highly recommend Nick and his agency to anyone who needs a great public relations strategy!"

Richard P. Hastings, Esq (Ridgefield, CT)

"Many people in business today are quick to make promises but fall far short when it comes to delivering. Nick Nanton is a guy that makes big promises and gets the job done! He is a master at what he does and will help move you to the next level in your profession. He is a guy that you need to get on your team! I am thrilled at what he did for me, and he will certainly be my go-to guy in the future! Thanks Nick for being the pro that you are and for moving me to the next level!"

Nigel Worrall (Kissimmee, FL)

"I joined the Celebrity Branding team at the Dicks + Nanton Agency for three specific reasons: 1) To become the leading authority in the US on vacation homes. 2) To be able to walk away with a book, a TV show and other materials I can use in my marketing efforts in the future. 3) To learn more about what I must do to grow my businesses; Florida Leisure

Vacation Homes, Total Real Estate Solutions and www.GoCruisePlanner.com.

The Agency promised me that he would deliver on all three counts and that I would have a great time doing so. At the time I was a little skeptical, but I took the plunge, and 12 months later, I can honestly say it has been one of the best business decisions I have ever made. Not only have I had a blast, but I have learned so much more than I had envisioned and have improved the revenue and profitability of my business.

The Dicks + Nanton Agency has way over-delivered on what they promised, and I have absolutely no hesitation in saying to other business owners out there that this is a "MUST DO," and as anyone who knows me will tell you...I don't use those words lightly. Thanks to the Dicks + Nanton Agency team...it's been fantastic."

Ron Caruthers (Carlsbad, CA)

"When we signed up to work with the Dicks + Nanton team, we were expecting to be exposed to ideas on how to get more publicity. We never expected the 'red carpet' treatment we have received. To say that we are pleased with the experience we've had with you would be a mammoth understatement. Not only have you guys worked with us on how to improve the branding of our existing business, [but] you have used your expertise to help us launch a franchise that will take us to a completely different level.

The Ultimate Celebrity Branding Experience® has proved to be an investment that has and will literally change our business and our lives. As you know, my partner and I have participated in 'coaching groups' for years; in fact, we run one for college planning guys, so we've seen just about everything in the 'we'll help you do... world." We can testify that you guys are hands down the best in the business.

You guys are awesome; keep up the good work. I feel like we're family, and if you ever need anything, just let us know."

Dr. Gayle Carson (Miami Beach, FL)

"The Dicks + Nanton Agency does everything they say and then some. If you want a team to rev up your celebrity status, these are the folks to do it! They have more ideas than most people, and best of all, they implement them."

James Brown (St. Louis, MO)

"If you are looking to promote your business and explode the growth, then come see these guys that can help you do that."

Tyrell Gray (Los Angeles, CA)

"When I first heard of the Ultimate Celebrity Branding Experience®, I was more than skeptical. I quickly realized that Nick and Jack are on to something huge. If you are a celebrity in your field, you are set for life, and the Ultimate Celebrity Branding Experience® is the shortcut to being the celebrity you want to be."

Traci Bild (Palm Harbor, FL)

"The Dicks + Nanton Agency has added that extra edge of credibility that was needed to take my business to the next level. I am confident that it's helped seal my position as *the* national expert on sales for the Senior Housing & Health Care industry."

Dr. Donna Galante and Dr. Paul Cater (Loomis, CA)

"Working with Dicks + Nanton Agency has been a first-class experience that will continue to pay us dividends now and into the future of our business, Cater Galante Orthodontics. The team at the Celebrity Branding Agency® truly care deeply about their clients and their clients' successes. Besides the definite benefit of growing your business, the relationships that you will develop with the other "experts" in your group will forge lifelong friendships and even business opportunities that are priceless. The investment in your "celebrity experience" is just that—an investment in yourself, your business and your future."

Jennifer Myers (Alexandria, VA)

"There is nothing better than the Celebrity Branding® experience with the Dicks + Nanton Agency to gain instant credibility as an expert in your field [and] go from a local expert to a national expert. This is hands down one of the best experiences to grow your business, and the team at the Celebrity Branding® Agency delivers on every promise they make...and then some!"

Jayson Hunter RD, CSCS (St. Charles, MO)

"The Ultimate Celebrity Branding Experience® and the Dicks + Nanton Agency have helped my business by teaching me how to be a celebrity in my own niche. I am able to gain exposure to a new population that didn't know who I was 12 months ago. The media exposure and credibility I have gained from this program is not only helping me now but will help for the future as well with everything that I do in my niche."

Dr. Vesna Sutter (Geneva, IL)

"I didn't know what to expect when I decided to proceed with this venture working with the Dicks + Nanton Agency. [I was] pleasantly surprised by everything; the organization was phenomenal. Very professional, very courteous, very friendly; made you feel as though you are the expert in the field that you do, even though you may not feel that you are, and [with] the confidence that they build, I'm ready to go conquer the world. So thanks guys; it was great and I can't wait to keep proceeding with this."

Donna Galante (Loomis, CA)

"Right after we did our TV show in L.A., Fox 40 News in Sacramento called us two days later, came in to our office, and did a live interview. So The [Ultimate] Celebrity Branding Experience is amazing; it's great for your business...I highly recommend it!"

Dr. Scott Schumann (Grove City, OH)

"A big thanks to the Dicks + Nanton Agency for all they have done to catapult me into being America's Premiere Cosmetic and Sedation Dentist. The masterminds and training are the biggest secrets to the success! SCHU BABY SCHU"

Nate Hagerty (Overland Park, KS)

"I'm simply blown away by the integrity, responsiveness, personal attention and RESULTS from the team at the Dicks + Nanton Agency. They helped my business achieve MAJOR visibility all over the world, but especially here in the United States, which forms the bedrock of my client list.

And not only is my information (written beautifully by his

team) 'out there,' but the search engine optimization factor for having my business be so authoritatively covered by major media outlets has ensured a solid foundation for any other web presence work my team and I undertake.

In short, I can't recommend working with their team more highly! (And don't be put off by Nick's fast-talking style—the dude is the real deal and simple extremely enthusiastic about what he does. Rightly so."

Andy Tolbert (Sanford, FL)

"When we first met Nick and JW, we were floundering a little with our training business…we had all of the pieces but didn't have a cohesive vision or strategy of where it could take us. Since working with them, we have put more systems into our office, we are looking at the marketing (and the results of that marketing!) in a whole new light, our website actually looks like a professional did it, AND we have an awesome vision for our company that will allow us to retire in just a few short years. Sometimes we get so busy in the day-to-day "stuff" of our businesses that we forget to stop and look AT our businesses, The Dicks + Nanton Agency has afforded us an impartial outsiders' view of our own business and the potential that it has."

Ronel Jumpp

"I want to thank Nick and JW for helping me make my dreams a reality. I came to them seeking advice for growing my business. Other people in the past have told me that my ideas and dreams for my business were unattainable. JW and Nick teamed up with me to brand myself and have opened doors that, in the past, were closed. They have opened my mind to seeing all of the different ways to make my business successful and to take it to the next level.

Thanks to them, today, I am in a position to achieve my business goals and am creating financial freedom for my family and my business partners."

Jon Ruhff and Yeosh Bendayan (Orlando, FL)

"JW & Nick have brought about more expansion in our business in the past three months than we thought possible. They got us to see the big picture while explaining everything along the way. JW and Nick took the time to understand our business goals and tailored their approach to us. We wouldn't trust our company with anyone else!"

CelebrityPress® Testimonials

Maria Struik (Bruce Mines, ON)

"I can't believe it: I am holding a hard copy of MY FIRST BOOK; a BEST SELLER! It is mind-blowing; I have to pinch myself to make sure that this is not a dream. You guys at the Dicks + Nanton Agency have over-delivered! Awesome, thank you! You did it; you put me on the Best-Seller list. Can't wait to see how this will impact my business."

Clint Barr (Brandon, MS)

Thank YOU! You guys delivered on your promise, and I'm honored to be doing business with you. Thank your entire team because they really greased the wheel to keep all the authors on task. And thank you for the opportunity to be a part of this entire process. My family, friends, and clients are all noticing my accomplishments and expertise like never before, and it's all due to the work you guys have done on our behalf to help make us best-selling authors. Again, thank you!"

Brian Horn (Pearland, TX)

"Just wanted to let you know that your book publishing service works! I was in a meeting yesterday competing for what would be a multi-million-dollar deal this year alone. Halfway through the meeting, I pulled out my book, "ROI Marketing Secrets Revealed" and gave a copy to each person. They were blown away! They decided at that point to give me the business and use the fact that they are working with a best-selling author on this particular project in their marketing. I had sold them on me, but the book was the tipping point that closed the deal. Best investment of my business career!"

Linda A.B. Miller (Southampton, NY)

"You all did an amazing job with everything surrounding the publishing and promotion of *Ignite Your Business. Transform Your World*. From the exciting launch event in New York City to the advice on and management of the promotional campaign to the awesome results—we're on the bestseller list!—I could not have hoped for a more professional and fun experience. Onward and upward!"

Brian Snyder (Pittsburg, PA)

"I would like to thank the Dicks + Nanton Agency for helping me become a "best-selling author." They made it easy and fun to write my book and were most helpful in the writing, editing, and publishing! I had a blast doing it!"

Jim Zaspel (Lansdale, PA)

"I can't fricken believe it! You actually pulled off even MORE than you promised me and the other authors of the book, *The New Masters of Real Estate*! When I heard your presentation on how you guaranteed that we would be on the Amazon Best-Seller list, I honestly didn't really think it was possible…BUT I trusted the guy [that] introduced us, so I got involved in your program on a leap of faith. Now that I AM a published best-selling author at the age of 24, I love handing out my new book to potential business partners, private investors, and other key business connections…you should see the looks on their faces!

This truly has provided an ENORMOUS amount of credibility that I otherwise couldn't have gotten. It's awesome! THANK YOU so much!

I really do hope that you pass out my phone number to anyone who is 'thinking' about getting involved with your agency. Not only did you guys OVER-deliver, but you and your entire staff were very helpful, responsive, and professional throughout this entire process."

Katrina Kavvalos (Sydney, Australia)

I have to say the staff at CelebrityPress® are the most professional, extremely prompt and organized people I have dealt with. They have been spot on with everything about the publication and release of their next book, *Relationship Age* (which I am so proud to be an author of). [I] can't get over how EFFICIENT the staff members are—thanks for being so wonderful."

Robert Skrob
Business Profits Radio

"Too many business owners are shy about promoting themselves as a celebrity. The more I study business, the more I understand that business success depends on your ability and willingness to portray yourself as a celebrity. This book provides a great roadmap for anyone to get started portraying themselves as a celebrity and attracting more customers to themselves.

"How many of you Tweet and Twitter? If you're just trying it out or doing your best to market yourself, check out Lindsay Dicks. She's the bomb.com when it comes to self-promotion."

Sallie Felton, Life Coach/Transition Specialist, International Talk Radio Host

#1 Best-Selling Author, *If I'm So Smart, Why Can't I Get Rid of This Clutter?*

"Like any vehicle, it will run smoothly **if** and only **if** 1) the right fuel is used, 2) you make it a priority to maintain it, 3) and you have a great mechanic! As a business owner, having your team in place is critical to success. I was happy with my original website; giving birth to it was a process. But after a while, as it grows, so do your needs. You change or your brand changes. It was not a coincidence that I met Lindsay Dicks from CelebritySites®; it was time...call it synchronicity at work. I had been rethinking my website and needed to delegate more of what I was choosing not to do regarding social media and web maintenance. I have never been so impressed by their professionalism, dedication [and] follow-through. They are there at a moment's notice to work through my questions, my ideas or concerns. I give them straight A-pluses. They have me for LIFE."

Dr. Chris Griffin (Ripley, MS)
The Capacity Academy

"It's always scary changing your website, even when you know you need an update. Lots of times you feel like you are on an island and the people developing your website could care less if they respond to your concerns or not. Not only did Lindsay and her staff stay in constant contact with me through the entire process, they responded immediately to each question and improved on my own ideas for the site. They thought of things that I would have never considered and have also taken my haphazard social media postings and formed a consistent strategy that is sure to blow the doors off anything I have done before. I feel like I have gotten many times over my money's worth already. Thanks Lindsay and team!"

Daniel J. Liebrecht
Clean Guru, LLC

"Want to hear *Ka-ching again?* Well, if your website's dead, not making money and you don't how to fix it—good news, there's an answer.

Call Lindsay Dicks and her staff at CelebritySites!

They simply know the 'stuff' you and I don't—important 'stuff' that actually works, creating a website that gets the phone to ring...and online sales to grow!

So humble yourself, *just a little,* like we did, and let these guys replace or revitalize your old *billboard*-type website with a dynamic marketing platform—one that's designed to 'pull' in sales in a completely different way.

It's more than a website—it's a complete, pedal-to-the metal, marketing strategy! And it's more than worth the little 'shot' to the ego.

One last thing…forget generalities—check this out! Our site was basically 'dead in the water' until Lindsay and her gang turned it into an interest-grabbing, marketing platform.

Now, we enjoy **first-page ranking** on not one but THREE of our main keywords. Our website went from an online brochure to a virtual *'living, breathing, marketing machine!'*

Yeah, we like the folks at CelebritySites.com a lot. YOU will too!"

Andy Tolbert

"I just got off the phone with a reporter for SmartMoney. com for an article about foreclosures that's going to run on AOL.com in about two weeks! She found me by searching on Google and found the press release you did that announced me as a new "expert" for AgentDirectNews.com. Then she went to my website and liked what she saw so she called me up! Imagine, being quoted in an AOL Real Estate story…you can't BUY that kind of exposure at any price! I knew I was making the right choice to work with you guys, and now that has been confirmed ten-fold! Thanks for all of your help!"

Brian Fricke, Owner, President

"**CNBC Contacted me because of CelebritySites®!** I just wanted to take a moment to say WOW! My last website took many years and many versions to never quite get what I wanted. In less than 30 days, you guys designed and built a brand-new website that I love, and now, not even 60 days since it's been live, I'm starting to get calls from television producers! Just last week I got a call from CNBC because they were searching for financial experts to feature on a new show they are launching and they found me thanks to my new website. This is incredible; thanks so much for the great experience. Anyone who isn't taking advantage of your unique expertise [for] Celebrity Branding businesspeople online is missing the boat in many ways!"

Yeosh and Jon

Push Button Productions

"Thanks CelebritySites®! With your help we just got picked up on a worldwide site for our music buffet option. They even put it on the front page of their site as a "breakthrough"! Our site, art and design, looks fantastic. Well done! We couldn't do it without you!"

ProductPros® Testimonials

Robert Granholm

ITArsenal.com

"Greg's experience is obvious when you talk to him. Our last coaching call translated immediately into profit; he gave me three actionable ideas, one of which was literally made me over $3,500 by the end of the following day."

Parker w/ www.learntogetgoodgrades.com

"Your ProductPros® system is simply awesome and a great

guide for anyone to get into business fast. Also, thanks for being a real person that I could call and talk to when I needed you!"

Derek Shannon

Body Fat Renegade

"Purchasing The ProductPros® System in late 2011 was one of the best things I have done for my online business. I spent about two months floundering on how to put an info product together and get it online. I had already published a book to Kindle that was going to be the outline but had no idea where to start. I was getting caught in the procrastination loop because I would look at the big picture. Fear and uncertainty would start to taint my thought process and I would go in circles. The ProductPros® System really simplified and clarified the steps that needed to be taken to start from scratch and actually get my product built and online. I would recommend this to anyone struggling like I was to get things going."

Mohamed Siduqque (San Diego, CA)

"One of the things that I've appreciated about your work— besides the intelligently articulated, valuable content—is that it is infused with integrity. It's obvious that you stand behind what you do; your rapid, personal reply to my email this morning underscores and confirms that. Thanks again, Greg."

Wesley David, Owner and Sr. Consultant

Crux Hosted Services, LLC

"Hey Greg! I love The ProductPros®. It's giving me the energy and drive to finally make some digital training that I've been wanting to for a while. Thanks for all you've done!"

Heather Torres, Department Chair, Entertainment Business
Full Sail University

"I had the opportunity to meet Greg Rollett when he came to guest speak to the students and faculty at Full Sail University. It didn't take us long to see that he is a forward-thinking personal branding expert. Greg displayed great energy and enthusiasm and truly engaged the audience by providing relevant tips and career advice."

Carlos Silva, Online Marketer

"When I had an idea of a product I knew what I wanted to do but could not "see" it, Greg sat down and created the framework with me, and as he was doing it, I started seeing everything. He not only opened my eyes but gave me the exact framework that was in my head; how he did that I do not know, but I do know he is an expert and on another level than anyone in this industry when it comes to product development."

America's PremierExperts® Testimonials

Kimberlee Frank (Oviedo, FL)

"Hi this is Kimberlee Frank, 'The Real Estate Junkie,' and I am writing to let you know how working with the Dicks + Nanton Agency made a difference in my life. First off,

I have shared the stage with a lot of people. However, it was always me having to impress my audience. Now, thanks to America's PremierExperts®, I have a long list of credentials that allows me to get on any stage. The media coverage was out of this world. The friendship with Jack, Nick, and Lindsay is something that cannot be replaced; we will always be connected. I have written many courses and wanted to write a book but never seemed to find time. With the help of America's PremierExperts®, they made it happen and not in years; everything was done in just 12 months. I just wanted to say, 'Thanks.' I couldn't have gotten this type of media coverage, book, and articles without your help. I would recommend this experience to anyone who is seriously looking to build their creditability fast!"

James R. Parrish (Fairfax, VA)

"Entering the final stage of the America's PremierExperts® program, I am in a great position to SHOUT about the outstanding nature of this program. I have been featured in national publications, interviewed by a top journalist, and will be appearing on TV in the very near future. The Dicks + Nanton staff know their stuff when it comes to promotion of persons and businesses. Trust me—you need to be one of America's PremierExperts®!"